Ian

Have a great
retirement

COMING IN TO LAND

RUNWAY TO RETIREMENT

By Keith Churchouse & Vicky Fulcher

© June 2022

Important

Further contact details and information can be found at
www.churchouseconsultants.com

No financial advice of any description is offered or deemed to have been provided within the text of this book. Seek financial advice from a qualified adviser for your own individual needs. We will not be liable for any actions that you take.

As this book is co-authored, it was a matter of debate as to whether we used 'I' or 'we' in the text. We've decided on 'I' in the main, although there is a mix of both.

We have also referred quite often to the COVID-19 pandemic of 2020 – 2022. Whilst we appreciate that this may date the book somewhat in years to come, for many people, it has been a life-changing experience, and a significant factor in their retirement decisions.

Contents

Special thanks

Keith and Vicky wish to send their thanks to both Rosemary Healing and Roger Churchouse for helping prepare this book by reading the many versions of our evolving text.

Foreword by Simon Culhane

As I am contemplating retiring after 40 years, I am exactly the person at whom this book is aimed and so I read this book with added interest. I wasn't disappointed.

At the age of 63, I am stepping down from my full-time role, because I believe that, ideally, one needs five things in life. 1) Health 2) Time 3) Purpose 4) Companionship and 5) Financial stability – and there is a golden period in life with the highest cumulative total. That's usually, but not always, somewhere between the ages of 55 and 70.

Retirement can last a long time and, with increased longevity, it could easily be at least half as long as one's working life, so it is appropriate that the book spends time challenging the reader to consider their personal motivation and plans. I completely agree that, for those in a relationship, the dynamics may change considerably post retirement and in my own personal experience, asking your partner "what's for lunch" isn't a great line to use!

This is a highly relevant, topical and accurate book which asks the reader to reflect and think. It does talk about money and finance but, as it rightly notes, it shouldn't be the primary purpose when preparing for retirement and it is Chapter 4 before the necessary financial technical details start to be explored.

This book may well benefit from being read over a series of days, rather than at one sitting. It is packed with information which is probably too much to be absorbed in one go and the questions raised at the end of each chapter are pertinent and stimulating, maybe requiring a conversation with others. And that's the point. Rather than being lectured at, the reader is encouraged to think for themselves and map out their own route and plans.

Part of the attraction of the narrative is its practicality with a down-to-earth grip on reality. The authors' anecdotes and experiences add to the richness and credibility of their suggestions.

The authors are right to point out the benefits and pitfalls of retiring too early – and there are financial, and possibly mental, disadvantages from doing so – as well as the benefits of financial planning (one of my five key ingredients), but they do so in a non-pejorative way, leaving the reader to draw their own conclusions.

I recommend that anyone contemplating retirement should read this book and preferably start doing so a few years before they intend make this significant life change.

Simon Culhane

Chartered Fellow of the Chartered Institute for Securities & Investment

April 2022

Note: Simon is Chief Executive of the CISI and writes in his personal capacity

Introduction

Congratulations! You've made it this far. Let's face it, it's not all been plain sailing, but you might have met your costs and liabilities throughout, looked after your loved ones, maintained a roof over your head and got a big dose of wisdom and experience to go with it. You've done OK and held it all together. There have been a few hiccups along the way, you know the ones, but all in all, you're not dissatisfied with all that's been accomplished. Perhaps with thirty years of work experience completed in your chosen expertise, you might with hindsight have made a few key changes on your journey, maybe there were a few missed opportunities, but no real regrets. And now it's time to look forward to the next decades of your life and the opportunities available for your retirement.

Referring to their view of retirement, a mature relative recently suggested 'I don't know what I want to do when I grow up!', with a smile on her face. Did any of us really grow up? Before you respond, I hope in part that the answer is no, because if not, we might have lost our sense of adventure, fun, freedom and excitement, all of which I hope you will have when you decide what your retirement looks like.

You would have thought that a clever group of now-trendy techno-nerds would have created an 'app' for retirement. Some claim to have done so, but this is usually just the money side of things, and these are not overly difficult, having built one ourselves. But it's not about the money, that's far too simple, and only one aspect of retirement. It's about you, and your life ahead is unquantifiable. You are sophisticated, intelligent, unique, and no fancy mobile app can truly represent all that is you. Perhaps we should revert to a more traditional form of communication, like a book, indeed this book, in whatever format you are reading it.

This book is not about money planning, although some financial thoughts will feature in the middle chapters. It's about planning the mental pathway, the process and the implementations required to reach retirement, whatever that means for an individual. You will see that we've added a few anecdotes along the way to add some flavour to the journey. Treasure the years ahead: they hold perhaps the greatest of life's value.

One key point to consider when reading this book is that we are all different, with different values both personal and financial, families, pastimes, health, faith, ethics, needs and desires. Therefore, pick from these pages what is relevant to you. The only thing we know for sure as authors is that you should benefit from some of the planning and experience, we have accumulated over the years as UK financial planners. The retirement 'menu' is as vast as that of the most sophisticated restaurant, and the variety of needs in what should be an exciting part of life is equally diverse.

In preparing our thoughts for the pages ahead, we reflected on what an average retirement, if there is such a thing, might look like. As our book title *'Coming in to Land: Runway to Retirement'* suggests, we look at the approach to retirement, and the age ranges we might target. These are the pre-retirement period, perhaps from age 50 to 60, the retirement point at 60 as an example, and the first decade or so of an individual's retirement era, when they are perhaps at their most active. However, what are the three phases of actual retirement that we have identified?

Three age and activity phases of retirement

From the age of 60, if you had 25+ years of life ahead in retirement, which might not be unreasonable if you enjoy largely good health, how do you see this from a holistic perspective? We don't want to hear 'a free bus pass with my State Pension' please!

All phases of retirement usually have different characteristics, and generically, what might they look like? Let's take a look.

1. 60-73 The active years

These might be the truly active years, encompassing the more physical pursuits of hobbies and holidays to suit your busy diary. Perhaps you will be difficult to get hold of whilst you gallivant across the globe or involve yourself in new interests.

I appreciate that an active 75-year-old might slam this book down at this point, noting their plan to go sky-diving tomorrow, but bear with me. After all, Captain Sir Tom Moore said, 'Life is to be lived and I've always believed that age is no barrier to living it.' He certainly accomplished much and brought joy and light to the UK during the dark days of the COVID-19 pandemic.

2. 73-81 The fulfilled years

A phasing-in of fulfilment and perhaps a slightly more relaxed agenda from the last decade or so might begin around this point. With many a pursuit, holiday or objective completed, the time to relax may have arrived, with more leisurely pastimes consuming the days and evenings. What's wanted will be treasured more, and what's not required may be discarded as time naturally becomes a somewhat dwindling commodity.

The needs of the family may become a more important feature of the calendar as you enjoy their company.

3. 81+ The chilled years

Health and wellbeing may now be an important focus, and the body may simply not do what you want it to do, or not at least at the speed that it used to do it, but the mind still prances like a 25-year-old. Much to reflect on and enjoy in comfort, perhaps with some additional personal care required. The family may also be more involved in keeping an eye on you and making sure that personal standards, whatever they may be, are maintained and enhanced where possible.

As enjoyable a time as the first two phases, but maybe at a slower pace in the chilled years. Health of the mind and body may well dictate the quality of life in these latter years.

Longevity is real

It might be easy for many to dismiss the possibility of significant longevity. However, the Office for National Statistics confirmed in their report of January 2022 that the number of people aged 85 or over was estimated to be approximately 1.7 million people, or 2.5% of the UK population.

This is projected to have almost doubled to 3.1m by 2045 (4.3% of the UK population). Significant figures and significant numbers of people living into the third phase of retirement.

These phases are only examples, and we will all know someone who breaks the mould. We love them for being like that; however, the majority might fit fairly well into the life phases noted above. In this book, we will concentrate on the lead up to and time spent in phase one and we will touch on phase two. Phase three, the chilled years, is a focus all of its own and indeed the theme for a future book.

There is no financial advice in the pages ahead, just experience of how people approach (or in some cases don't approach) retirement, the assets they have, and the transition that they make from their frantic working lives to a new time or phase when they slow or stop work, to a time of fun, time, travel, and hobbies, subject to their health. Sometimes referred to as 'Woofies' (well-off older folk), we need to be sympathetic to the fact that the baby-boomer generation (1946-1964) and the older end of Generation X (1965-1979/1980, growing up during the sometimes-turbulent Thatcher years) may enjoy more financial security than the younger generation, who are trying to meet all their liabilities (mortgage, family and so on) with more limited resources.

Our text focuses on those around age 50+, who need to start to turn their attention to the next chapter in the book of their life. I have reached the age of 55 and feel personally involved in the mix of what to look for in helping others to come in to land for retirement.

If you were on stage at an hour-long production of 'This is Your Life', the lights and cameras were on, and the final section was being read out by the compere, hopefully with fun, love and exciting tales, what would they say for you? You will see over the course of this book that I do not advocate very early retirement, as I do not believe this is good for the soul and mind (or, quite often, for the pocket). Whatever age you select to end, or slow down work, make sure it's what you want and what you can afford, if possible. The answer is that the final section of your 'show' has not been written yet, but you have full control of how it reveals itself.

As a financial planner, I am used to asking probing questions about people's lives, which can be slightly awkward in social situations. When the tables are reversed, I discovered I can get a bit spooked. Recently, I was asked about my plans for the future. Sorry? The questioning is my gig, not yours, I thought, as I was quizzed about what I might do, and plan, and where…and the point was, with whom? For me, it was like being back in the playground, being asked, 'can we play games please after school?'. The person asking was actually sounding me out to see if I would be around to keep them company in retirement, and it was interesting to experience this approach.

All the usual open questions I hope will come flooding through about your time after work: Who with? Where? Why them, there? How much? What to do? Are there parameters, even restrictions (perhaps your health)? You will get the gist of this thinking, and each point will need to be answered or at least guided into position. You could of course just let it all happen, but there might be less enjoyment in working this way. It's a bit like taking a holiday and landing at an airport. The pilot knows where to line up with the correct runway, what speed they will be doing when the wheels touch down, how heavy the landing will be, and on which carousel your luggage will appear. All need to be agreed before you set off.

What are you passionate about and what's going to give you passion in the future? There are those that might think that I have already framed this book incorrectly, especially those who promote retiring as early as possible. You have seen them in the national press, fairly advocating the wisdom of their ways in their prudent management to reach a retirement goal, perhaps a decade early. Well done to them! However, my experience is that most do not work this way, making other life choices to meet their own and their family's needs. I also question the potentially negative effects on the brain of stopping work early. The majority of individuals want to get the most out of all they can achieve from their business or career. Remember that an individual in good health could live to their mid-eighties plus, actuarially speaking, and over half a life not working by retiring very early does not ignite my passion. But that's me. More importantly, what about you?

Minimum retirement living standards?

Before we go further, it may be helpful to reference what someone really needs to put their feet up. We all have our own lifestyles, and have different incomes and expectations from retirement, whatever that looks like. A report from October 2021 from Loughborough University and The Pensions and Lifetime Savings Association suggests that a single person will need post-tax annual income of £10,900 net for a minimum standard of living in retirement.

The minimum retirement living standard covers a typical retiree's basic needs plus enough for some social activities, such as a week of holiday in the UK and eating out once a month, but does not include running a car.

That spending budget increases to £16,700 for a couple, the calculations for the study suggest. For the first time in the assessment, Netflix subscriptions and items such as haircuts are included, and it's an interesting read to compare your lifestyle with what they have as an average.

Financial calculations for retirement living standards are pitched in the study at three different levels - minimum, moderate (approximately £20,800 pa for single person to £30,600 pa for a couple outside London), and comfortable (approximately £33,600 pa for single person to £49,700 pa for a couple outside London), - and are developed and maintained independently by the Centre for Research in Social Policy at Loughborough University. For those living in London, the income need rises as you might expect in each of the three ranges, by about 10-20% pa.

You can make your own view on how these indicated retirement income levels might fit with your view and expectations of what the future might look like. More on the report and how the averages on what's been counted in average household spends in retirement can be found at the study website which is: www.retirementlivingstandards.org.uk

Much to take in

We will cover significant ground during the pages of this book, and there is much to take in. Some nice to know, other points vital to the overall process of the important business of your retirement. Don't fear the 'R' word, embrace it! The more you know about it and about you, the better.

On reading this book, if all it does is to stimulate the mind that there is a time ahead when you will not be working, for however long that will be, that you will need enough money to see yourself through, and that it does need some discussion and planning, then it will have been worth the time spent.

Your personal journey through life has been unique and this will not change as you move into retirement and beyond. The next phase of your life - and note please that I did not say final phase - will also be personal to you and a reflection of you.

Simply put, make it yours!

1. Limbering up your retirement thinking

You may have thought it would never arrive, but here you are aged fifty-plus and coming to the realisation that you will actually retire at some point. You are not alone, with millions of others like you across England. Over 10.8 million people in England fell into the age range category of 50-64 years old, according to a recent survey (July 2021 – source: Statista.com).

I know from conversations with clients, colleagues, professional contacts and friends that many of us feel we are still aged around 25 when it comes to our abilities and attitudes. We have a 'yes we can!' approach, with a view that we still have a full range of opportunities ahead of us, and that we will leap from our beds every morning to tackle with vim and vigour whatever the day has to offer. The reality might be quite different after the age of 50, but I hope for you that many days are still like this. Don't misunderstand me; it's not like life and enthusiasm has ended. Not at all, but it might be a bit blunted.

In this chapter, we are going to do some warming up of our minds to look forward to the issues, attitudes and challenges we all face as we approach the factors surrounding retirement. We'll start by looking at some of the emotions and feelings that need to be considered, before turning into the money side of things, and then bringing it all together.

You may remember when your parents were the age you are now, and you thought they were *so old*. Well, guess what, you're there now! Your children probably now think the same of you! And perhaps the most important question for you is,

'Am I going to be OK?' Financially, it can sometimes be a discussion about how to carve the financial 'cake' rather than whether there is actually a cake to carve. For others, the position may not be so rosy, and continuing to work may be the only option to make ends meet. Perhaps the pressures of work have meant that you have not found any real time to give it a thought. One contact who worked four days a week confirmed in a call on a Friday that they do their 'life-laundering' at the end of each week to catch up with their administration and finances. We all work in different ways.

One question I would pose to you at the outset is 'Would you do it all again?'. We will look at this further in the book, so be ready. Proof is personal, and your life is proof of who you are.

And did the pandemic change your view? Two years of relative chaos mixing up the flight paths of our lives and plans, set against political malaise, followed almost immediately by an invasion in eastern Europe. Stolen years for many.

Statistics produced by the Office for National Statistics and released in March 2022 detail that the number of people aged over 50 moving from employment activity to inactivity, with the main motivation being retirement, rose sharply on the arrival of, and during, the pandemic. A real 'brain-drain' of business experience in many sectors being lost in quick succession.

In addition, the economic climate they may retire into seems to be shifting and one possible financial signal of this is inflation.

Inflation returns!

Most people have not really needed to factor in rising costs to their future income planning over the last few years because rates have been rather benign for the last decade or so. You might remember from yesteryear that this has not always been the case. I hope that when you cast your mind back to your childhood and teenage years, you remember fun, Wham! and the Live Aid concert, rather than any concerns over the UK's monetary policy and high inflationary costs. This section is not designed to be an economics lesson, but it's helpful to understand how inflation might work before you retire.

Simply put, an inflation rate is the measured rise in the price of an item or service over a year's period. Many economies use a basket of commodities to measure an index, such as the Consumer Prices Index (CPI). Prices don't have to rise, they can also fall, which is referred to as deflation, or stand stubbornly still. This can lead to 'stagflation' if high inflation persists and is combined with other factors, such as stagnant demand and high unemployment. However, inflation over the last decade or so has been historically low and flat. When economies restarted, or at least tried to, after the Covid-19 pandemic, inflation returned and very fast. Central banks across the globe have watched this, and some have taken measures to try to quell the position. For example, the Bank of England quickly increased its base rate from an all-time low. Tragically, war in Europe reared its head for the first time in a generation when Russia invaded Ukraine, pushing prices of food and energy even higher.

The key point here is that inflation is no stranger to UK shores: just look at the 1970s, 1980s and 1990s. Indeed, the low rates we have seen over the past decade or so may well be the stranger, with inflation rising at the time of writing. There are no guarantees on future positions but building in some protection against the long-term effect of your real purchasing power (after inflation) is seriously worth considering. You might want high income at the start of retirement but leave a margin to cover future cost increases as and when they arrive.

There! The first economic part of the book over, and more about you to follow. I am sure you might guess that there are more 'financials' to come later, which is all part of the retirement tapestry, and a cornerstone of the book's objective of helping you land safely in retirement.

The real you

The real you is not all about facts; how you feel is just as important.

There is a rule in UK retail financial advice that you should 'know your client'. This is not unreasonable, and therefore when looking at your money planning, you're likely to be asked twenty questions about yourself and your circumstances. These notes, usually in a form, are likely to gather the 'hard facts' about you and your circumstances, such as family, house, salary, pension fund values, investments, health situation and so on. This ticks a box for a regulator but is unlikely to show the real you. Indeed, on its own, this line of factual questioning edits out most of what makes you an individual.

It's the 'soft facts' that really show who you are, how you got to where you are, why you made those choices, and importantly, why you are making the life choice in the near future to retire. If you think about the big decisions in your life so far, you might have thought about which university to go to, who to couple up with, who to uncouple from, which career path you took. Each painted a part of the picture that is you now. Each was a life junction that sent you in one direction or another. Retirement is no different in being a major life junction, and perhaps involves some of the most significant decisions and directions you will ever take.

If you looked at the soft facts about you, what would you note down? Perhaps it's worth it as an exercise.

Please do think hard about what you want to achieve and why, because sometimes things get in your way. It's never too late to revisit some of the opportunities you thought may have been lost.

Lost your mojo? I did!

I remember that about age 50 I lost my motivational 'mojo' somewhat. The magic and charm of life rather dissipated into the ether, and I was not expecting it.

I don't look forward to birthdays, especially big ones, and these milestones weigh on my mind. Not for any reason other than that once the time is gone, it's gone. I have often said that the most valuable commodity is time, rather than money. Money can be saved, or earned, or replaced in certain circumstances. Time cannot be stopped and is always spent.

I remember starting in the financial services industry some three plus decades ago, meeting new individuals and undertaking the client fact-find process to find out all about them. I used to work out how much older than me someone was every time. You can guess that as the years have ticked by, that now rarely happens, with the converse calculation now applicable. Does this matter? To me it did and was simply another signpost on the conveyor belt of life that time was ticking by and could not be replaced.

There was no reason for losing my drive at that time, just that the usual trials of life were weighing down as the business continued to move forward. It took around six months to have a more positive outlook, and this has thankfully stayed with me since. The magic returned, although I remember being angry and frustrated whilst the difficult period lasted. I am sure this is not an uncommon tale, although I appreciate that this may not be the case for others. As age creeps up, I find that the risk of the day-to-day tribulations of life dragging on your spirit begin to grow.

Perhaps some controversial thinking coming up. I believe that the risks to personal wellbeing increase the earlier you retire. In my opinion, those who advocate stopping work before age 55 as a minimum may find the real personal wellbeing cost greater than the assets and fund values they have accrued. With perhaps thirty years in retirement to think about whether you got it right, the toll can be high if you get it wrong. Working longer shortens the retirement time odds, but I believe extends the wellbeing.

Keeping your mind stimulated and challenged throughout the process to retirement, and into retirement, is vital for a healthy and happy few decades ahead. Moving from a busy work life into long, empty days is nobody's idea of fun, and we have seen the damaging effects of this on the mental health of individuals who have retired (often somewhat involuntarily) without planning what they wanted retirement to look like.

Keeping your motivational 'mojo' in retirement is entirely possible – however, you need to be aware that enthusiasm can be lost and needs to be nurtured throughout the decades ahead.

With these initial warm-up thoughts complete, we hope that you are ready to begin your journey. Some may find that making a few notes along the way might be worthwhile, even if they are simply to jog your memory.

Your nudge notes

To help, you will see that at the end of each chapter we have added a notes page for you to add your thoughts about the topics raised in the text. This book is about you, your approach, your plans, and your feelings about coming in to land and retiring.

We all have different dreams and aspirations, along with different financial and social backgrounds.

Don't be shy in jotting down your own opinions and plans as we go through the text, indeed your text.

Your nudge notes:

Coming in to Land – Runway to Retirement
Chapter 1: Reflection on where your years went

Your thoughts and views

- Are you energised by the thought of retirement, or do you have to work up to the topic?

- What has this chapter revealed to you about your situation and how you got there? Why?

- Could you let go of work straight away, or would you need time to make the journey to retirement? How long would you need?

- What challenges past and present do you face in your life that are revealed from this chapter? Can technology now help you?

- If you could change one thing to improve your lead up to retirement now, what would it be?

- Write down one action that you will now implement.

2. What do you expect to happen?

What was the one thing that woke you up to the fact that retirement exists and has your name on it? If you work for a larger organisation, your employer might have sent you on a retirement course or seminar. Can you imagine that invitation dropping in your inbox? Bang! There it is! The first signal to get ready. Others will have been ready for years, and some will never be prepared to retire.

The thought of retirement or even semi-retirement is not an option, or even a preference, for some. In our experience, this might be because they never saved, never believed they would live that long, or more positively, enjoyed their work so much that they did not want it to stop. However, life happens, and time disappears, and here they are facing an age when it might be effectively forced upon them. Over the years, very sadly, we have witnessed a few individuals cry at the thought of finally leaving their desks and putting their pen, overalls, licence, or calculator away for good. They had no plans for this, and therefore no plans for the immediate future, which creates fear...and tears. We indicated in Chapter 1 that this difficult situation may be avoided if proper plans are made. One contact said that he was, after accumulating some wealth, going to do absolutely nothing! He was really looking forward to it.

You will need some cerebral capacity to be ready in yourself, so clear some mind space and let's look at what needs to be understood. Overthinking needs to be controlled, as you will see.

Over-thinking in bed

Do you ever find yourself lying awake at night, almost every night overthinking, being troubled by this, or challenged by that? You really should not own these issues, but your mind presses the start button in the middle of the night, and you have no choice. Sounding familiar? Philosophising at 2am through to 4am, then finally getting some rest and waking up shattered is never good. However, the odd gem can come from a wakeful night, and one suggestion is to have a note pad handy to scribble out any winning answers. Write it down and then clear your mind.

Personally, I can normally hang on to two points in a night, but when I get to three, I have to get up and write it all down. This is one thing I will not miss when I retire and look forward to my body's natural clock phasing out this insomnia.

Different styles and approaches

We all have different styles and approaches to life and the way we go about it. Controlling or laissez-faire, direct or shy, traveller or home focused, a sofa lover or an athlete, or more likely a combination of some of the above, and lots more besides. Understanding what type of person you have been and perhaps who you will be in retirement is an important step in your journey. Will the leopard change its spots, or continue to be decidedly leopard-like in retirement? What does your partner or spouse expect the real you will be when you return full time to them from the combat of your work life? Have you talked about this with them?

Looking at personality traits further, you might tend towards being either a natural spender or a saver when it comes to money. We meet many couples where the individuals are at either end of this financial spectrum, somehow giving balance to each other, although not without a raised voice or two at times. We can all change, although thirty plus working years of managing your money to a particular level is unlikely to see an individual move away drastically from where they are. Setting the scene and managing expectations in your own mind of where you are and where you want to be is important at the outset of planning for retirement, at which point you may have more time and perhaps less income.

This variance between individuals is also usually reflected in the financial information we gather. Some have paid off their mortgage early, used excess income to build up cash savings, have little pension, and no Will. Others are still mortgaged, no immediate savings, good pensions and a Will. As a financial planner I have experienced the whole spectrum of financial snapshots and the personalities behind the positions. I am honoured to share their lives and to help them forward as they look towards retirement. You never know what you will find as they come towards the end of the accumulation phase of life, perhaps with a little further to go before they look at using these assets for the next phase.

Of course, it is good to look at the financials. However, these money details tell no story without their owners, the people themselves. We add to this mix their views, opinions and attitudes and the life story begins to come alive. The lead up to retirement can be an emotional time, especially at the thought of ending work, but what is it for you that will spark your emotions at this time?

Constraints of children gone

One client noted that her daughters, who spanned a six-year age range, were now on the path to leaving home. The youngest had reached 19 and had now left for university, with the older daughters having left university and now in rented accommodation close to their respective workplaces. The juggling of work and family life, or 'the balance' as our client called this era, was coming to an end.

She felt that she was rather rattling around in her home but was enjoying the newfound freedom of having the place to herself. She was happy with this, knowing that her children were never far away from a hot meal and the washing machine if needed, and was concentrating on what she wanted to do for herself into the future. Work continued, but the end of this was also in sight and the ability for her to focus on what she really wanted to achieve was growing. She was excited by the prospect, having enough assets to meet her long-term needs.

The change of the children leaving was significant, and part of the process of evolution and transition from one lifestyle to the next. The constraints of looking after others had diminished significantly and some release of responsibility had occurred. A life junction? Perhaps not, but a significant development as part of the continuous conveyor belt of life.

What will you most look forward to stopping? And why?

Work will stop at some point. Let's not underestimate that this can be a very emotional time, especially if you have served in your current capacity for a number of years.

The week when the goodbyes, the final signing out emails, collection of your faithful and aged coffee mug to be returned home, the leaving lunches and a celebration cake will arrive. I am not sure they give away gold watches any more, very seventies! Will you be ready for this tangible departure?

The thought of this fills some with dread. For others reading this, they would have thrown the keys at the boss at the first opportunity.

Whichever way you feel, what will you look forward to ending? The answer to this will be truly personal and only you can answer. Make a note of it and ask yourself why this answer. Perhaps it should be the top of your list of things to avoid in retirement?

What will you miss the most? And why?

Conversely, looking at the flip side of the note above, what will you miss the most? For me, I think it would be the routine and structure of work. It gives me a framework to maintain some control and I like that: something I will need to build into my retirement planning when I get there. I have no plans to retire yet, having just committed to a new ten-year office lease, but that should not stop me from looking to the future and what it might hold.

What about you? I am not referring to missing the 'hygiene factors' of a salary or car. Maybe you will miss the camaraderie? The commute (perhaps not)? Wearing work attire to suit your trade or profession? The cerebral challenges of your accumulated knowledge and how could this be re-applied in your retirement if you wanted to? The coffee and cakes? This list could be endless, and I hope there are a good few positives on yours, but again, worth making a note with the aim of building this into the plans for the future you.

Letting go or a busy fool?

There is a point when you are going to need to let go of work, but for some this is not as straightforward as it might be for others. Commitment to an employer, or to your own company, is admirable and usually necessary to move forward; however, immersing yourself entirely at the expense of your personal life can be damaging and alienating to those you hold dear.

It's hard to avoid the tensions of work, and these can weigh on you personally. Indeed, some people become so involved in their role or business that they lose sight of who they once were.

We tend to see two extremes of this situation. The first is the individual who has given all they possibly can to their role, and has taken on more and more work, and simply can't see a way out. Perhaps an employer leaning on your goodwill to meet their targets. The second is the person who over time has used work as a way of avoiding conflict with family or personal issues, sometimes unconsciously, often deliberately. A busy or misguided fool?

No one can judge, but whatever the reasoning, the end result can be similar, in that retirement is perceived to be much further away than it actually is and is seen either as a far-off dream, or as a threat to their continuum on the distant horizon. A sterile existence for some, but not uncommon.

Being a 'busy fool', as they say, will not delay the inevitable fact of retirement. To be blunt about it, unless you want to spend your last breath at your workplace, there will be a point when you stop work.

What is going to welcome you each day when that happens? As noted in the section above, what do you actually enjoy, and with whom do you want to enjoy it? If you can't remember, or you don't want to think about it, you are by no means alone, but you can't bury your head in the sand for ever. Take little steps at first to extricate yourself from the workplace to give you time to know what will really work for you in the decades ahead.

Hand over with pride and check your notice period

You are likely to need to have a hand-over period once you have given notice of your retirement. You might need to check the terms of your employment contract to see how long a notice period you must provide, especially if you have been with an employer a long time. Six months' notice is not uncommon for long-serving employees and directors, although notice periods will be lower in some other roles. You may - correctly - have great pride in your work and your personal contribution to a business, and you might want to give the business as much time as possible to pass over your work to someone new. Your replacement is probably not going to have the skills and in-depth knowledge of the business that you do, but that makes it more important to give your best at the last and leave with your head held high. Some companies will keep some retiring key staff on a retention contract for a period after retirement, just in case their historic expertise is needed. One person I spoke to said they had declined such an offer because they would no longer have the control and oversight that they had in their previous role. It was nothing personal, just the way they liked to work.

Life is not a spreadsheet

Some people feel that life can be run through a spreadsheet. For some, the spreadsheet becomes their life. Asset values, investments, income, outgoings, costs, pensions and so on are analysed and tested almost daily to check that all is in order. Perhaps it's their business training and experience that makes them focus in this way. It is difficult to break away from this regime, and sometimes very frustrating for their partners, as we have been informed on many an occasion. 'Them and their bloody spreadsheets' was one exasperated comment.

Making sure the money is in order is a good thing, and to some this becomes a hobby, tracking fund performances as an example. There is however more to life than a spreadsheet, and there are advisers who can help you look after these things to allow you the time off you deserve.

Be careful here. We have seen some who have become consumed with fund performance, charting every aspect, and sometimes missing the big picture by trying to micro-manage. Their health has suffered when it needn't have. By all means, enjoy the tables and stats, but keep it under control, because markets do not always move as you might expect. Where you can, hand it over, close your PC or laptop and go and plan a holiday instead. You will know if you can afford to.

The best-laid plans...

For some, retirement does not work out as originally anticipated. One person we know had planned from his age of 25 to retire at age 55. He had mapped his working life entirely around this view.

Life, work changes and divorce got in the way, and his plans evaporated. At age 50, the pitter patter of tiny feet had arrived at home following his second marriage and the subsequent birth of a daughter. He was thrilled! His work plans had changed and thinking of his daughter's age, his instinct was to protect her through her education years, whilst also helping the older children from his own and his new wife's previous marriages. 70 years old was now the new target for retirement, noting that this was not a chore because he enjoyed his work.

To me this illustrated how the circumstances of life can change so completely and the needs of others can up-end your own plans for how and when you had originally expected to retire.

I remember my father retired for the first time round on his 50th birthday. This was in an era when the minimum retirement age to draw pension benefits was lower than the current level of age 55. He carried on working on a consultancy basis for an additional decade, whilst also drawing his pension. Halcyon days indeed, especially in the 1980s. His early retirement set a perceived target date for his children to see if they could retire from their first career at the same age. I have clearly ignored this 'lesson'. However, I think I enjoy my work more now than he did then.

Your nudge notes:

Coming in to Land – Runway to Retirement
Chapter 2: What do you expect to happen?

<u>**Your thoughts and views**</u>

- Well, you made it this far, but what's going to spark your emotions about retirement?

- What will you miss most about the end of your work? Why?

- What will you miss least about the end of your work? Why, and how will you avoid it in the future?

• What have you taken from this chapter to suggest that you are ahead or behind of what you expect to happen at retirement?

• How does your spouse or partner and your family feel about your retirement? Are they ready to have you back full time?

• Write one action that you will now implement.

3. The ocean of time ahead of you

When things are going well, what gets you up in the morning energised and ready for the day? What's that going to be in retirement?

The urge to compete in the workplace may have ebbed as you reach the highest level, rank, or position that you can accomplish through your abilities. There are of course those rather annoying individuals who seem to get promoted to their 'highest level of incompetence' as one contact put it recently. There always will be, and you tolerate them where you can with a veiled grimace. Sure, you will not miss them when you retire, and can look forward to claiming back some of the cerebral energy that they may have consumed. Any negative work issues can be replaced with positivity as you plan your release and the way forward. And, of course, any work positives can be built into your new retirement life.

My wife joked recently that if I ever stopped work, I should return to my first job as a paper boy! I laughed, but then thought about it. I am a morning person, up with the lark, and am unlikely to break this habit. As an aside, everyone should recognise if they are a morning, afternoon or evening person and use this to their advantage. As a paper boy, I could go through the newspapers and current affairs early every day, as I do now, get some exercise, and say hello to a few people along the way, before being home for breakfast. I am not sure I will rush to deliver papers when I stop work, but a routine of this nature has its appeal in giving some structure to a retirement life.

But what to think about?

Where will you retire?

Just because you worked in or commuted to and from one town or city does not mean that you have to stay in that location. Are you a natural urban dweller, or do you seek space, the great outdoors or perhaps the coast, here or abroad? Think it through because this might be one of the only times you have left to explore alternatives. Does your partner share the same view or passion for where you should both spend the next decade or so?

There may well be influences, such as family and friends, that may sway your geographical preferences, or it might simply be climate, preferring to live full or part time abroad in warmer climes to help health and mobility. If you plan to do this, check out what UK benefits that are currently available to you, if any, may be lost if you move abroad permanently.

One idea some have is to rent for an initial period before committing to a purchase to make sure they have chosen the right location for them for their future.

All these factors need to be accounted for to be able to truly settle in the future.

What will you retire to?

Do you have a burning desire to achieve something before you feel you may be too old? I am not referring to a personal 'bucket list' here, but perhaps the opportunity to build your own home, write a book on your life story, run a small business, or to be a local councillor or church warden, as examples. This list is as varied as us all and perhaps it's just as simple as improving your golf handicap and having the time to perfect your swing.

What will tick your box?

Community

Years ago, I moved to a house in a semi-rural village on the outskirts of a town, historically wedged in the commuter zone for London. Thirty-five minutes on a train every day to Waterloo seemed a fair price to pay for the promise of a higher salary. Often this does not prove to be the case.

We had kept ourselves to ourselves for many years and were then invited to a garden party organised to welcome 'new' neighbours. We were asked when we moved into the village, and it was not our intention to appear unfriendly when we noted that we had arrived some eight years ago. It was however a reflection of a busy life and the time that working schedules consume. Village and community life was there to enjoy – we simply did not have the time.

When working, that choice may not be in your gift, but when you stop or slow work down, the opportunity may return, and you may want to grasp it. Being part of the local community can offer great social benefits for all and knowing who can help where is usually worthwhile.

Why now?

Please don't answer this question with the response, 'because time is running out'. It's not, although the GP might start to introduce some medication to keep you going. However, choosing your timing carefully is important because the scope to recover from life errors may be rather more limited. Medical science, along with social mobility, has moved on dramatically since your parents were your retirement age. We are better educated, better informed and in better health than most other generations before us. This is in part why we live longer than in previous times, although we are suffering from more cognitive issues, such as dementia, in later life, than earlier generations.

I hope that the decision for you to retire will be achieved naturally. You will know when it's right to go, and I hope that the trigger is a positive one.

When taking action, do it with conviction in your heart that your time has come to start the next exciting episode of your life.

Content in your own skin

When referring to life and its outcomes, I often note that you make your own luck. Some snatch defeat from the jaws of victory, whilst others seem to achieve great things effortlessly. Perhaps it's a confidence thing, or just a bluffer's guide to life in general, and you will know which camp you usually fall into.

You know the type of person that you get on with, and who gets on with you. You have been building this understanding from the time you formed your initial social skills and developed and tested these at school. You know who to avoid being stuck with at a party, and those that attract you as an opposite. Each is different, perhaps with different ethics and values. You don't have to understand them completely but knowing the differences can help you understand who you are and what you like. It's a bit like the wide range of newspapers available in the UK: each attracts a different readership, and you will know the stereotypes of each and how one group views another.

Being content with your life and your lot can be hard to achieve. Knowing what contentment looks like to you is a good start, and it's then a case of how far you need to travel to reach that destination. Perhaps a look back in order to move forward might be helpful. When was the last time you were content, and when, where and why was this?

What is your favourite decade so far?

This might be a difficult choice for some people. Perhaps it was the university years and starting out on your chosen career path? Or when your children were growing up? Or the recent years during which you have enjoyed business success, or promotion, or house move? Each of us will have a different answer.

If you can answer this question fairly easily, what was it about that decade that made you particularly happy or content? And what happened to change that – why did this happiness change or fade? In retirement, will you be able to re-discover, or re-invent, what you had to bring you contentment? Where were you located during these happy years, and is that where you want to retire to? More on these topics later in the book.

If you can't answer this question, perhaps your best is yet to come in the decade ahead? How exciting, knowing that it is down to you to take control and make it happen. Taking this further, there is the conundrum of the meaning of 'paradise' if it exists in retirement? Like others, you might have given up on the dream of 'paradise'. It's not lost, as such, it just no longer seemed achievable when the realities of life kicked in. It got pushed down the agenda and then onto a second page, never to be considered again, until now. Retirement might give you the chance to get closer to the dream of what life might look like for you when you first thought about being set free from bringing up a family, or from work. If you had been able to achieve your every wish already, you would probably not be reading this book, so managing expectations may be advisable. Nevertheless, striving to achieve your dream now might be one of your last real chances to achieve your goals.

Life's side effects have value

Change of any kind can be difficult to accept, especially as you get older. We get into our routines, our likes and dislikes, based around our abilities, desires and budget. Generally, the current position that you enjoy, or otherwise, is an adaption to your surroundings as you make your way through life. It is your evolution.

Personally, I can think of key times that were pivotal in my life to where I am now. As an example, I started a company at one of the lowest points of my life. 'Creek' and 'paddle' spring to mind (you can guess the other words) and the options to move forward were limited. However, the change was part of who and where I am now, and this personal evolution remains a huge part of that change. More importantly, that shift, along with running a business for nearly two decades, has many side effects that do not sit well with me. I am uncomfortable about my tolerance of friends and family, which is poor, my questions are direct with limited small talk, my decision making is sometimes quick and harsh, I hardly laugh any more, I work, work, work and find switching off highly over-rated. It is easier to turn the boiler of my brain down to simmer to get back to the boil quickly, than to really let it cool and take a break. Oh, and I discovered that writing is hugely cathartic. My wife is very understanding of me, and my writing, and this support should not be underestimated.

These notes are not a sob story, just observations and a reflection of unintended, or perhaps unexpected, side effects of making a change to a life. Overall a very positive change as it transpired. Perhaps this might resonate with you in thinking about your life events that have brought you to where you are today. Take a moment to think about it. Some of the side effects that I have noted above are on my list of what I would like to correct when I finally stop, if it's not too late for them or me, although I am very comfortable with the hardened emotional armour I have on for the rest of my business journey. Will you have similar personal items on your list that you plan to adjust when you retire?

Most of us will have become accustomed over the last few years to making adjustments to life. We have all seen major disruption to our lives because of the pandemic and our emergence from its effects. Holding onto past strict routines and structures has at times been impossible. After two years of unwanted evolution, it is clear that some do not want to return to the past. In the main, I do not sit in their ranks, but which is better? The old or the new? We can all spot the problems with the old, and changes that needed to happen, but the new world, with virtual engagement, working from home, hybrid working and so on has more than a few wrinkles to iron out.

As I have mentioned, we have just moved the company into a new office which some might suggest is outdated in itself. We created a 'Zoom Room' area for virtual meetings, which I really like. Designed and bespoke for virtual meetings, it is really effective and gives me confidence when seeing people online. It simply would not have happened three years ago, but now seems only natural.

We can and do all adapt, and retirement is a change in our life where adaptation will be a key part of life for a year or two as we find our feet in the next chapter of life's story. Do you remember going to big school for the first time? Fun times, I hope. It might be a bit like that, just with more money and responsibility and when you fall over in the playground, it hurts a lot more!

Nothing at all

If your work life has been rather frantic in its general make-up, the thought of doing nothing at all might sound like the best news ever when coming to retirement. No need to hurry to get up, no need to go to bed at a reasonable time, because there is nothing to get up for in the morning. A sedentary existence, at least for a while, might sound fantastic.

It is uncommon in our experience for someone to respond in this way when asked about their plans for retirement. However, some certainly plan nothing for the first few months, just to catch their breath from the end of work. The deliberate segmentation to take this rest period is to some extent understandable, but it can't last forever. Some might disagree, but you will need something to channel your energy, if only to keep mentally and physically fit and agile.

The age you retire may define what you want to achieve. The age you retire is your choice, and a recent survey reveals some of the effects.

Targeting an early retirement age, say 60 years old

You may already have an age in mind at which you plan to stop work. This might be guided by a parent who retired at a particular age, and you want to match or go earlier than them because of their subsequent reaction. They might have had a fabulous time in retirement, or it might not have been quite so rosy.

To give this example retirement date of 60 years old a little more context, Aviva, the insurance company, undertook a survey on early retirement planning with the results released in December 2021. There were a few statistics that made interesting reading, as follows:

- 17% of those who had taken early retirement headed for 60 as the age to exit the workplace.
- 25% of those targeting early retirement were working towards 60 as the age to leave work.
- Of these, 32% were 'wanting to enjoy more freedom while still physically fit and well enough to enjoy it' as the primary factor for aiming for an early retirement.

Finally, financial security was the second most quoted reason for going early, effectively being able to afford not to work.

Importantly, from a wellbeing perspective, the Aviva survey also revealed:

- 68% of people who retired early said that their happiness improved as a result.
- 44% of early retirees said their family relationships improved.
- 57% said that early retirement had delivered a boost to their mental wellbeing.
- 50% said that early retirement had delivered a boost to their physical wellbeing.

(Source: Aviva survey: December 2021 / with thanks to Aviva for permission to quote this survey)

All strong responses to a retirement survey, I am sure you would agree.

Planning is key to adding structure to your way forward, and remember, this is your journey. Have a think about when you want to go and why. Some of the responses above are compelling. However, you might have your own personal reasons to select a particular age or junction in your life.

Do you really want to go early?

We highlighted in the introduction the possible three phases of retirement from age 60 through to the third phase starting at age 81+. It is important to bear in mind your likely longevity when considering your retirement date.

Retirement for many reaching the age of 60 is likely to last 30 years, if not more. In our opinion, two factors come into play here: firstly, have you built up enough to fund your retirement, or do you need to work for a bit longer to make things more comfortable? Secondly, is there more you want to achieve in your career before throwing in the towel? It's far easier to continue working than to retire and go back to work, although we have significant experience of individuals who have achieved this successfully.

Your nudge notes:

Coming in to Land – Runway to Retirement
Chapter 3: Ocean of time ahead of you

Your thoughts and views

- **Does the length of time ahead excite or hinder you? Why do you answer this way?**

- **Where do you plan to live in retirement and why?**

- **What inspires you now and what will inspire you in retirement? Why?**

• What have you taken from this chapter to suggest that you need to adjust your thinking of retirement?

• You might think that the time ahead is not enough for your needs. How are you going to bring structure to your time in retirement, particularly when you consider the three age phases?

• Write one new action that you will now implement to help your preparations.

4. Starting to get your ducks in a row

All life plans take time, and retiring is no different. So far in this book we have considered the emotional and personal aspects of the lead-up to being ready for retirement. You will know that anything important that you have achieved in your life took planning. Perhaps a sprinkling of luck as well, but mainly actual work. You did not get where you are overnight, it was a progression that you directed over time, twisting and turning as life invariably does. You will steer the next phase of your life as well; you've just got to take the controls.

Recognising that retirement might be a feature on the horizon in your life is important from age 50 onwards. It can be an earlier or later age but acknowledging it's there is the key point. What that looks like is up to you and planning for it is key. It might even take some gumption to pluck up the courage to address the end of your working life.

So, how are you going to look at it, because your life cannot be really detailed on a spreadsheet or bar-chart, but will take thought. The money side can be calculated, but your feelings, desires and emotions are not to be underestimated, as we have seen. You will appreciate that you are not alone, with many of your friends, family and business colleagues treading carefully around the retirement abyss, aiming not to fall in too soon. Share with them, discuss what you're thinking about and how retirement could look for you. See what they're up to; they might have some interesting ideas and you may well find some unexpected companions with whom to enjoy existing or new pastimes.

Starting the process of retirement planning only six months before the date planned is, in my opinion and experience, not the best way to approach such a momentous change, either financially or from a personal adjustment perspective. Retirement planning takes a lot of cerebral 'bandwidth' to match reality to expectations. Therefore, if you have the focus, start a good one or two years beforehand as a minimum.

What was your trigger?

Something will trigger for you the start of the retirement process. This might be out of the blue, or a natural progression through your life. For some, retirement was accelerated by the two years of Covid-19 problems over 2020 – 2022.

In this latter example, the furlough scheme put in place during the pandemic may have been the catalyst to start retirement, especially when the initiative ended. Being parked up from work for a few months on eighty percent of salary was enjoyable, affordable, and sustainable. When the call to return to work came, the thought was rather unwelcome, and the idea of stopping work for good looked more and more attractive.

Regulation of financial services can be tiresome, but one helpful recent initiative is the sending of 'wake-up' packs by pension providers to pension holders to start putting the topic of what your pension might look like onto the agenda. It can work very well in giving a gentle nudge to say, 'Hey, you need to look at this!' in an easy-to-understand format. You will see in Chapter 7 that this is one of the reasons why you should keep in contact with your pensions.

We make no apology for starting to steer this chapter, and indeed the next two chapters, onto the topic of money and money planning. Some might feel the urge to put the book down at this point, but we thought we would start with some basic 'house-keeping' stuff just to warm you up. And we appreciate that money and financials are pretty dry topics, and sadly often overcomplicated by those who should know and do better.

Gobbledegook

Doing money stuff is not the most inspiring thing for a lot of people. Some clients take on an adviser or advisers that they trust to take the strain out of managing their finances. They never understood, had no wish to become immersed in the financial process and they are not going to learn now. The technical jargon was all gobbledegook, they felt. 'That's what I've got you for' has been said during many a meeting. Good advisers are honoured to share their clients' trust, noting that it is a significant responsibility over many years or indeed decades in some cases.

Tedious though the subject of money may be to some, it is nevertheless necessary and in this and a few other chapters, we have aimed to capture some of the things to consider. If it gets a bit heavy, then park it up and return when your mind is fresh. It might take a few visits but give it a try. Believe me, you are not alone if you glaze over even at the thought of looking through your retirement plans.

Money planning can seem intangible and possibly unachievable on your own, that's why many people avoid it. However, your life is very tangible, so what can you consider in combining the two aspects? How do you map out what you want to achieve in retirement? Let's have a look.

The canvas of your life

I am not sure that 'retirement' can be tangible when being hypothesized. However, drawing it can be, and visualising a plan can work wonders in making the picture real, as we have experienced on many occasions. Using a diagram, like a timeline, that you can revert to over time works well. And why use just a sheet of paper? You can use the reverse side of a wallpaper roll that can be extended out over a lounge or dining room floor and your future life plans and intended experiences can be noted down in large scale. Simply draw a plan line down the middle, ascribe equidistant gaps for the years ahead, pour a glass of something delicious and start adding notes, dreams and dates, preferably with your partner if you have one.

You're not going to get it right first time and it's going to take time. Let's not underestimate the personal value of the plans and desires that you are drawing out. If you are achieving this with your partner you might find out a few things that you never knew. Positives, I hope. And you're probably not going to get it all down on one night; after all this is the canvas of your life, and we know most great paintings are not completed in a day, even a week. So, when you reach a good junction, stop. Roll it up, put it away safely and then roll it out again when you are ready to add more. It's your canvas and your plans, so add to the mix as you prepare for the future.

When you are satisfied it's complete, reference it when needed and please do keep it reviewed, adding where you need to, and perhaps ticking what you have done. It can be a really powerful tool to share with your loved ones as you move into the different phases of retirement.

If you were to think of 'Base Camp One'

Money planning within retirement should not be like climbing Everest. There are going to be some challenges to conquer, the odd slip here or there, and certainly some basic financial planning that you might want to implement. A bit like reaching 'Base Camp One' before you start your ascent to the retirement you anticipate.

I have listed a few basic money planning points below for you to consider before we get into greater detail in the next two chapters. Hopefully a gentle start!

Checking your State Pension online

It is well worthwhile checking your State Pension online and keeping a record to ensure you are up to date. This benefit usually offers significant value to an individual's core income, and if you have a partner, the doubling up of pension incomes can make a real difference. However, this income alone is unlikely to be sufficient to give you a good living standard in retirement.

Shortfalls do occur and hence the reason why you should check every few years, usually online, although there is a paper form available. Where appropriate, if there is a shortfall, you can normally top up and this may be a good option for a guaranteed income that is anticipated to increase each year.

Those who may not have worked, or worked only part-time, whilst they cared for children may well have claimed Child

Benefit. This had an additional benefit of ticking a National Insurance contributions box to give credits for each year they claimed. This will add to the State Pension years required for a full State Pension (now 35 years for those with no qualifying years before 06 April 2016). It is worth checking, though, to ensure that all is as expected and do keep a record of the results.

Emergency deposit fund, or EDF for short

No, we're not referring to the French energy company.

Life throws up calamities on a regular basis. They seem just around the corner, and if they are not, the fear of unexpected and usually costly hiccups can haunt an individual anyway. Maintaining a buffer of readily available cash, or near cash holdings, is usually worthwhile. From a negative perspective, to cover the unforeseen, and from a positive, to cover an impulse buy that happens to come up.

As an adult of any age, you might want to think about maintaining three to six months' net income as a suitable buffer in case of need. Of course, many survive on less, and some will want more. However, the concept of having some in reserve at all times is usually sound. Life will continue to throw up its challenges in retirement, either personally or for your loved ones, and being financially able to smooth over life's wrinkles can add real peace of mind.

Debt free?

Entering retirement debt free is preferable to most people we meet. Retirement is a life junction to throw off some of the shackles of the past. Paying off accumulated debt where possible and cost effective is usually a sensible consideration. Mortgages, loans, credit cards and car loans may all feature on the debit side of a person's financial balance sheet and getting these under control at the point of retirement is often favoured.

However, attitudes to when a mortgage should be repaid have changed over the last decade or so. In the 1980s and 1990s, property loan terms were normally curtailed by the standard retirement age of 65. I wonder if lenders were accused of ageism, because this no longer seems to be the case, with some people working longer, and some lenders taking pension income into account. I understand that mortgage end dates of age 70, 75 or even later are now not uncommon. It might be helpful to have this flexibility, although whether this is a worthwhile option, if available, is for you to decide.

The feelgood factor of being mortgage and debt free is often noted in our experience as one key milestone to achieve. The thought of owning your own home outright is a comfort for many. Take your own individual financial advice for your needs from a suitably qualified adviser, noting that tax free cash released from a pension may be a source of capital to help in this regard.

Scams!

Please do look out for financial scams, or for those promising high returns from dubious or obscure investments. The mantra 'if it looks too good to be true, it usually is' should reach across all you do.

Do check who you are dealing with, both the individual who is advising or guiding, and the business or product involved. You can normally visit the website of the UK regulator, the Financial Conduct Authority, to check their register, and you can also have a look on the Companies House website if you are dealing with a limited company.

Allow time to implement your plans

If you are taking advice with the plan of implementing your retirement requirements it is worth noting that it might take a month or two to get all the paperwork and transactions complete. During the pandemic, this time frame was sometimes extended. From a cashflow perspective, if your salary ends one month and you want your pension income to start the next, make sure you leave enough time to allow the implementation process to go through.

Also, if you leave work on an agreed date, it may take your employer two or three weeks to make the final payment into your pension fund from any deduction from your last salary, along with their own contribution. This may delay drawing your benefits for a period to ensure that you have the full amount available to you when accessing your fund.

Making a Will and Power of Attorney arrangements

Making sure your estate is in good order with an up-to-date Will is important and a cornerstone of any financial planning. You should seek advice from a suitably qualified legal adviser in this regard.

You do not want to die intestate (without a Will) and leave your loved ones to clear up the financial mess, because I can assure you, they will not thank you. You may at this stage also want to at least put on the radar the future need for Power of Attorney arrangements, and there are two types: health and wealth. At this stage of your life planning, you may have experienced the need for Power of Attorney arrangements for elderly relatives, and your own situation will be no different.

Also, please ensure that someone you trust knows where these documents are held in case the need arises. We once had a situation where an individual was fully affirmative in noting that she had a Will and that it was up to date. On her sad early death, her spouse took around a week to find it, filed away safely, with much angst caused during the search.

Please be ready!

Your nudge notes:

<u>**Your thoughts and views**</u>

- **What was the trigger for you to really start thinking about retirement? What do you fear the most?**

- **What will you write on your future life canvas for your plans, dreams and aspirations?**

- **How much of an emergency deposit fund do you want in retirement and why that figure? Have you checked your calculation and shared this with your partner?**

- When will you bring all your paperwork together to start really looking at the money side of things, as we will do in the next chapters?

- Have you thought about scams and are you ready to spot them? Be careful.

- If you could change one thing to improve your future plans now, what would it be? Why?

- Write one new action that you will now implement.

5. Show me the money!

You will have seen in the last chapter that we have started gently on the topic of money and the way you might want to consider and plan in preparing for your retirement.

You may be surprised that, as financial planners, we have got this far into a book focusing on retirement without launching into the finer financial details that will need to be considered. To return to our aeroplane analogy, you should also be aware that each person will approach their retirement flightpath at a different angle, speed, and trajectory. It certainly varies our own working lives in helping bring them all in to land. Bringing together the money and the emotions as to why an individual needs to achieve an objective is fascinating.

You do not have to be a particular age to retire. You can retire any time you want, but if you are relying on a pension plan to give you the financial freedom to do so, 55 years old is normally the minimum age by law to access your pot, or pots, with a few very rare exceptions. This minimum age is planned to rise to age 57 from 2028.

And if you are going to retire, you're likely to need money behind you to enjoy your time. Let's also not forget that for many people it's a very 'British thing' not to discuss money. This is something that has been noted in the press in recent years, particularly within families who keep their cash questions to themselves. There is even a 'Talk Money' week each year in the UK in November. Retirement, and the lead up to it, is an ideal time to get talking about all things money related.

What does the word 'pension' mean to you? As a financial planner, you might expect me to suggest that it is a tax efficient financial product that pays a regular income for the rest of your life. If your attention wandered just reading this, you are not alone. Pensions are not the most exciting topic!

It might be fair to suggest a 'pension' is an asset of any kind that can provide future benefits in retirement. It is fairly common for us to see individuals with a few sources of capital available to use in later life. In principle that could include property (commercial or residential or both), investments, business assets, pensions, the State Pension, gold, even cryptocurrencies. For many, their 'pension' is just the use of assets that they own to pay for their future needs. Property can provide rental income or cash on sale, and a business sale can provide capital or perhaps continued share ownership that generates dividend income. We will detail a few of these opportunities in the following pages.

Let's look at a few generic things that you might want to consider as a high-level approach to your retirement runway and landing.

Trade jargon and possible plan changes

We have already mentioned technical jargon in the last chapter as this can often be found within financial services. I have aimed to avoid this where possible. Inevitably, though, there will be terms and product types that you will need to understand when manoeuvring your existing arrangements to start paying pension benefits.

You might well need to make changes to existing investments and pensions to move them from an accumulation (savings) phase to an access of funds phase. Many newer style plans offer such flexibility, although older plans may well be more rigid in their structure. This should not be an opportunity for 'product flogging', perhaps like it used to be when you first started work way back when, but for well-planned changes to existing arrangements to meet your needs and aspirations as you move forward.

As you might anticipate, trade jargon and a historic mistrust of financial advisers is not helpful. Indeed, a lack of financial advice for pension savers risks destroying the flexibilities offered by the pension freedoms introduced in 2015, according to a report in January 2022 from MPs on the Work and Pensions Select Committee. The modern financial advice industry bears little resemblance to that of thirty years ago, and it is pleasing to note that historic attitudes and poor outcomes are fading, and the real value of good financial advice is increasingly appreciated.

Getting good advice or guidance on your arrangements should be a priority.

Unhappy about your trajectory? Get a second opinion

An individual can get guidance and advice on their money plans from a range of sources. Some charge, others don't, and a lot depends on whom you trust. It's good to talk to find out what can be achieved and what's available.

Most of us have walked away from an offer or purchase in the past because it just did not feel right. Make sure that you are comfortable with the advice and guidance you are receiving. If not, don't be shy in getting a second opinion elsewhere, almost a sense check, especially for the big decisions you are about to take. This second opinion may re-affirm that you are on the right lines, and all is good, or save you from an expensive error.

Where are your pension funds now?

You may well know what pension plan amounts you have, but do you know where any funds you have are invested now, and if they match your investment risk and appetite as you head towards the retirement exit? Many people think that they should take lower investment risk in retirement, and if that suits their updated profile, that's fine: for example, if you plan to buy an annuity. More on this later in this chapter. However, if you do not know how you want to draw pension benefits, then your future investment term could be the rest of your life - which as we have noted could be a decade or two, or even three. Therefore, check the investment risk you maintain now, to see if this matches with where you want to be.

It should be noted that many workplace pensions (and some personal pensions) will alter your investment profile on a set course as you approach retirement. This is sometimes known as 'lifestyling'. You might want to check if you are part of a programme like this in your pensions to see if it meets with your individual plans looking forward.

Ethical, environmental, social and governance (ESG) investing: where is your money really?

The section above comments on the need for investors to be aware of investment risk but does not touch on the issue of what the money is really doing.

The effects of the COVID-19 pandemic and our recoveries from it will last for decades to come, indeed perhaps the rest of our lifetimes. Attitudes in many respects of life will change as we settle down to the new normal (sorry to employ this vastly over-used term). Importantly, within this change will be a focus on the ethics of where our money is and what it is really doing to, or for the global environment and humankind. Of course, this then raises the question, 'Where is your pension or ISA (Individual Savings Account) really invested?'. Perhaps the tougher question is, 'Do you care?'. More and more people are keen to ensure that their investments are invested for good, whatever that looks like to them, or at least to try and make sure that the companies they invest in aren't doing active harm to people or the environment.

Ethical investing is nothing new. However, from the historic days of it being an unusual choice of investment strategy, the market has moved on well and there are good funds out there showing consistent and firm returns over the medium term. Very encouraging, although, as ever, we must add in the caveat that past performance is not a guarantee of future performance.

An evolution to this positive process is the emergence of ESG investing. ESG screening helps to identify funds which align with an investor's objectives and motivations for investment, whatever their personal preferences may be. Funds can be invested in the home market, or overseas, to suit an investor's attitude to and tolerance for investment risk. The momentum for this process had started prior to the pandemic. It could be fairly argued that perhaps its timing was excellent, noting the sea-change in attitudes that may prevail.

However, this is my take on the current situation, which some may argue is outdated. The main issues are marketing 'noise' in trying to sell products, and potential greenwashing. Greenwashing is effectively dressing - in this case investment funds - to make them look environmentally or ESG friendly and attract you to invest your hard-earned cash, when the reality may be different. This is of course disappointing and has, I believe, led some to delay implementing an ESG investment strategy until the position from fund managers and their assessors becomes clear.

We have also noted that in our experience, many investors are keen only to allocate a proportion of their funds to ESG investing. Almost a 'try before I buy' approach, with any potential proof being achieved in future investment reviews, in the form of returns, or ESG impact, or indeed both.

To be clear, there are some good ESG focused investment funds available, and these are fully accessible. However, the maturity of this market, when the possibility of greenwashing should be minimal, may take a further transition to evolve fully.

Income tax!

Yes, your pension income is subject to the standard income tax rates. You have your personal allowances as normal in retirement, but the income received from the State Pension and other pensions is subject to tax at your highest marginal tax rate. Most individuals have a nil rate income tax band that lets the first thousand pounds or so a month of taxable income be paid without the deduction of income tax.

A payment from a private or employer pension is normally taxed at source. This means that the pension provider collects a tax code for you from HMRC and pays income and the associated tax charge based on this coding. Tax codings can change dependent on your personal tax circumstances.

The State Pension is paid gross, meaning no tax is deducted, but the income is still taxable. Therefore, if you have other pension income coming in and the State Pension starts, it is not uncommon for the other pensions to be taxed more heavily through a change in your tax code. If applicable, you might want to look out for this update when this change occurs as you may find income from your private pensions goes down as the income tax is collected from these.

Use your annual tax allowances where you can

There is a myth in the UK that the tax system and the annual tax allowances are not particularly beneficial. On an annual basis, the tax allowances available to individuals are not that large. However, if used where possible each year, the real value can mount up and be substantial if the financial planning programme is maintained. Just ask the 2,000 or so ISA millionaires reported by the press in early 2022 after a freedom of information request to HMRC.

Each individual has annual tax allowances which are valuable and can be effectively used to reduce taxation on your income, pensions, and investments now and into the long term. Please do take advice where you can, or do your own research, to see what's available and to have the potential to gain extra tax efficient value.

Managing expectations: what to expect?

With some generic financial points noted above, let's have a look at what you might expect from a pension asset and the way pension benefits can be drawn. The points below are examples only, and normally you can have a 'mix-and-match' of these options to suit your individual needs.

What might I get from my assets?

There are often differences in asset classes, and differences in the ways that each type of asset can provide benefits in retirement, whether this is in the form of income, capital gains or both over time.

As an example, a residential buy-to-let property might produce rental income whilst owned and capital gains when sold. Stocks and shares might return a dividend income and again capital gains, although neither the income nor the capital gain is guaranteed from most assets. Working against these potential returns might be management costs for a property and charges for an investment plan. Of course, let's not forget the effects of inflation.

And the timing of each gainer, or indeed loser, in the examples above may not be correlated. Therefore, one reasonable question might be whether property or investments are better? And there is no set answer to this because it depends on the time period in which the question is posed. In our experience, many individuals sit in one camp, property or investments, rather than both. You may well have a view as to whether you prefer property or investment, or you may be someone who is comfortable to invest in both.

Whilst the capital value of property may have a lower correlation to stocks and shares than to some other assets, it is likely that you will find some similarity in the returns that can be expected from property and investments. Dividend income from UK shares might average between 2-4% per annum as a very rough example, and rental income (after management costs) could be about the same, noting that each property opportunity will be different. Each income stream will vary and will have its ups and downs. As an example, UK dividend income largely slowed during the pandemic period, but has mainly recovered at the time of writing. As a further example, if a property is left empty, there will be a void rental period, which may well reduce overall returns significantly. One recent enquirer who had three rental properties suggested that they 'hated being a landlord', citing in particular sporadic income and no end of bother and anxiety. Conversely, there are others who are very satisfied with their position as a landlord.

There have been many studies over the years to try to identify a sustainable level of income over the long term from a pension asset. At one point, an average of 4% of the fund value per annum was considered to be relatively sustainable. It's not an unreasonable rule of thumb but should be kept under review. However, each client is different and with many pension plans allowing significant flexibility in the timing and amount of income drawn, the choice as to what is taken may vary each year. As an example, some individuals set out to take a high draw from their pension funds with the aim of extinguishing the overall pension value over the shorter term. This objective might be driven by income tax planning to use the personal income tax allowance each year, as an example. This strategy would normally be supported by additional assets or income streams to call on in the future once the pension in question is extinguished.

Income for the rest of your life

It might be fair to suggest that if you knew the date and time of your death, you could plan your money, and how long it needs to last, more easily. Of course, we don't know, and this is where planning ahead can really help. As we saw in the introduction of this book, living to age 85 or 90, or longer, is not unreasonable to anticipate. This might give you a long time to spread your money out and you might have a varied array of assets that can be used to provide income in the future.

For those who do have pensions, and there are lots of different types, I have detailed some headlines as to how pension benefits might be used, noting that there is no individual advice in these pages.

Final salary type pension scheme

If you have a final salary type pension scheme, the final income paid will normally be defined by your salary at leaving service (usually increasing in deferment), your length of service, and the accrual rate used by the scheme. The scheme administrators will also take into account any debits if you divorced and passed some pension value to your ex-spouse. Final salary type pension plans are sometimes called defined benefit plans because the benefit is defined at the end. You can usually take some tax-free cash, and again the parameters of how much this can be, along with the minimum, are usually defined by the scheme rules.

You can speak to the scheme trustees to see what you have, and a full response can normally be provided at no cost to you once a year. Invariably, these types of plans are no longer offered in the private sector, with companies generally now offering auto-enrolment schemes or personal pension arrangements. These are usually not so generous.

Money purchase and personal pension plans

Alternatively, or alongside other schemes, you might have a money purchase type plan. This effectively means a fund that has a value that you can draw on. You might see terms such as a personal pension plan, additional voluntary contribution (AVC), or self-invested personal pension (SIPP) as examples of this type of fund. However, the list of names used extends a lot further once the marketing teams have had a go.

We will now look at this type of pension plan further, in terms of both characteristics and how benefits may be drawn.

Money purchase and personal pension schemes

The principle that a pension should provide you with income for the rest of your life does not change. Significant rule changes occurred to pensions law, enacted in 2015, which could be viewed as changing this position by giving greater access to the pension pot available. This change saw a significant drop in the use of pension annuities (lump sum purchase of income from your fund for the rest of your life), although they can have their value, as you will see.

These pension changes were largely welcomed at the time, although there were fears that some would go out and blow their pension pot on a Lamborghini sports car. I think a few did!

However, as a principle, the day you take your pension benefits does not change the day you die and with good longevity now generally expected, it is important to take a balanced view for both now and into the future as to how a pension pot could be accessed.

With this in mind, the 'headlines' that should be considered by each individual before they make any important pension decisions are as follows:

- Normally 25% of any undrawn pension fund can be drawn as tax free cash. More on this later.
- There is no restriction on income levels that you can draw from your plan.
- Income can be phased to meet your needs.
- Any income taken is still subject to income tax. You should be mindful of higher rate income tax charges if you take significant sums from your plan.
- Under current legislation, there is no tax charge to beneficiaries on your pension fund on your death before the age of 75.
- Death benefits for beneficiaries of those who die aged over 75 will be taxed at the recipient's highest marginal income tax rate, whether taken as a lump sum or as a regular income.

In addition, you no longer have to purchase an annuity at the age of 75, which was a requirement years ago. It is important to remember that rules and regulations for pensions, like most things, can and do change over time, so check before you take any action.

Can I draw my pension and keep working?

Yes, you can draw your pension and continue working. This allows individuals to take their benefits in full or in part whilst continuing to work, maybe part-time, as they move more gradually to retirement. You may want to consider any effects on your income tax if this is the case, as the combination of earned income and pension income may increase your overall income tax liability. Look out for restrictions on continuing to pay into a pension whilst working and drawing a flexible pension.

Drawing pension income

There is no limit on the pension income in retirement that can be taken, although if you exceed specified levels as described later, there may be additional tax charges. The pension benefits that you will receive from your personal pension depend on the fund values finally available.

You can choose the type of income/benefit you take. This could be:
- To draw tax free cash and take the balance of the fund as cash (or a proportion), subject to your highest marginal income tax rate.
- To draw the tax-free cash and leave the remaining fund unchanged.
- To purchase an annuity.
- To phase your retirement by purchasing annuities/taking income on a year-by-year basis with segments of the overall fund while leaving the remaining fund invested.
- To take income from the invested fund on a year-by-year or ad hoc basis ('flexible drawdown').
- Combination of the above.

I have provided some thoughts on these options below, noting that you may finally choose a combination of arrangements.

Annuity purchase

One common historic way to take retirement benefits under pension plans was to take a tax-free cash sum and use the balance of your fund to buy an annuity. An annuity is a level or increasing income for the rest of your life and is taxed in the same way as salary. The fund used usually dies with you, although you can add in some guarantees at a cost.

Annuities may well have their day again as the preferred option for providing retirement income in years to come but have not been popular over the last decade or so.

At the time of writing, annuity rates in comparison to rates available thirty years ago are low. This is in part because mortality rates, the information on longevity that actuaries usually produce, have improved. In simple terms, that means we are living longer and the older you are, the higher the annuity rate you get. Also, amongst other factors, the assets that back annuities to give them their guarantees of income, gilts (government stock), do not offer high returns in the current economic climate. If inflation, and possible high interest rates return, we may also find annuity rates increasing. In our experience, annuity purchase is currently rare. However, times and attitudes can change.

An annuity gives you payments at stated intervals, say monthly or annually, normally until your death, although you could buy fixed term annuities if needed. You give your pension fund either to the insurance company with which you have built up your funds or to another on the open market to purchase as large an income as possible for the rest of your life. There are annuity comparison sites available to detail who's offering you the most income for your cash in your circumstances. There are several types of annuities, which include Guaranteed, Value-protected and Impaired Life Annuities if you have a poor health or smoker history.

If you like the sound of an annuity, then please do shop around to get the best deal, either directly, or through an adviser. Buying an annuity from the company that holds the pension may offer poor value, so do research the market. Before you do, if you have an older pension policy, perhaps first established in the 1980s or 1990s, check if it has any valuable guaranteed income contained in the small print. Some do, and an example would be guaranteed annuity rates, which can have significant value.

Guarantees & dependants' pensions

The cheapest annuity you can buy, i.e., one that will give you the highest starting income in return for your pension fund, is usually one that pays a level income on your single life for the rest of your life. However, when you die, no further income is payable even if you die after receiving only a few income payments.

At a cost, you can add extra benefits to your annuity at the outset, and these can include a guaranteed period of say five or ten years, which will ensure income payments continue for the fixed period after you buy the annuity, even if you die straight away. You are also able to purchase an escalating annuity which will mean that your income increases in payment and may help keep pace with price increases and the effects of inflation.

Where married or in a civil partnership (or with a financial dependant), you may decide to build into the annuity a spouse's pension that will continue to be paid in the event of your death. Typically, the pension will reduce by one half or one third in this event, as an example. This might be a standard feature in a final salary pension scheme but check your own circumstances.

Guaranteed annuities simply purchase an income based on the annuitant's age, normal life expectancy and the level of gilt yields (on which annuity rates are based). These guaranteed annuities may be improved upon for 'impaired lives', which are subject to medical evidence, because of reduced life expectancy, and this is an area where there could be an improvement in the basic annuity rate available at the time.

Advantages of an annuity

- You can choose between a level or increasing income for life.

- The income is guaranteed to be payable for at least the rest of your life. Alternatively, you can purchase an annuity for a fixed term.

- Your pension income can be guaranteed for a certain period so that payments will continue for a fixed period after your death.

- If you live a long time, you may get back more than you used to buy the annuity in the first place.

- They are relatively simple plans and usually do not involve on-going planning.

Disadvantages of an annuity

- Annuity rates may not be favourable when you buy your annuity.

- The amount invested is gone and the value received from the plan dies with you or with a spouse/ dependant on their death.

- The levels of income and annuity features selected are fixed at the outset and cannot be changed even though your future income requirements, personal circumstances or health may change. The annuity will not change with your changing life.

- It is possible that if you die early, you may not have got back the amount of money you used to buy the annuity.

- Options selected at the outset, which come at a cost, may not be used in practice e.g., if you choose a spouse's pension option and your spouse predeceases you then the cost of this benefit has been lost.

With these points noted, what is the alternative, noting that you can have a bit of both if you prefer?

Income drawdown

By using an income drawdown facility, you can normally take tax-free cash, usually 25% of the fund, and the remaining value would be used to provide a flexible, taxable income, if you choose.

Originally, pension income drawdown contracts had some restrictions. There was a cap on the income you could take, and some older plans still maintain this cap. This was in a way a legislative protection from an individual taking too much from their pot. Back in April 2015, this annual withdrawal limit was removed for new money purchase/personal pension schemes. There is now no limit on the amount of income you can draw. As you might guess, taking high levels of income can be risky, as one of the issues associated with income drawdown is that if the underlying fund does not perform well and the plan charges are high, the future income could be lower than if an annuity were purchased now, or indeed the fund could run out.

If no income, or minimum income, is taken, there is a far greater opportunity for the fund to grow and, if you opt for an annuity in the future, it is likely that its income may be higher because you are older. However, you would have to bear in mind that you would not have enjoyed higher income in the previous years. Financial advice costs, both initial, and for ongoing annual reviews, also need to be factored into the retirement income costs for the future.

Any income provided from an income drawdown plan, whether capped or flexible, will be taxed at your highest marginal income tax rate.

There are risks involved in income drawdown, and some of these are as follows:

- The fund may not grow as hoped and this could lead to an eventual shortfall in income in later years.

- Annuity rates may fall further in the future and if an annuity is eventually purchased it could be lower than if one were purchased now.

- If maximum income is required, this route may well not be the most appropriate as the growth needed to maintain this income level could prove difficult to achieve.

Death benefits

One of the main attractions that income drawdown may have is the superior death benefits.

If you buy an annuity, then it is simply on your life/joint lives and there would usually be no return at all to your estate on your death beyond the guaranteed period that might be written into the contract. With income drawdown, the residual fund is available.

If you die before the age of 75 whilst taking income drawdown, or if the fund is uncrystallised (no tax-free cash and/or income yet drawn), your beneficiaries will be able to receive the value of the remaining fund tax free.

The person or people receiving the pension will pay no tax on the money they withdraw from that pension, whether it is taken as a single lump sum or accessed through income drawdown.

If you die over the age of 75, the beneficiary will be able to access the pension funds flexibly, at any age, and will pay tax at their marginal rate of income tax.

Pension income drawdown therefore gives you and your dependants far more flexibility in making use of the pension funds. However, this is given at a price and the price is that you lose the guarantee that is provided by a conventional annuity.

If you choose this option, you might usually expect to nominate the fund to your financial dependants in the event of your death. This nomination can be updated, if needed, in the future.

A big pension pot, or combined pots

If you have saved hard into a pension for your retirement, or into various pensions, then the total value might be quite sizeable. Dependent on the value, this might in itself cause a problem with additional tax issues.

There is a pension 'Lifetime Allowance' (LTA) for the maximum amount you can build up in pensions whilst still enjoying the tax benefits. The LTA is currently £1,073,100 (tax year 2022/2023 and planned to remain frozen until April 2026). This limit has fallen from previous peaks around a decade ago of £1.8M, reducing over the years. If benefits over the LTA are taken, a Lifetime Allowance tax charge will apply, i.e., you will have to pay tax on any excess over the allowance limit. Any amount above the LTA can be paid as pension income (taxed at 25% in addition to your normal income tax), or lump sum cash benefit (taxed at 55%).

Testing of your benefits against the Lifetime Allowance will be carried out each time you crystallise an element of your pension savings. How benefits are drawn will have an impact on how they are valued. Don't forget that there is also an additional LTA test at age 75 for your personal pensions, based on current legislation.

If you are affected by these issues, you may want to seek individual financial advice on the timing of drawing any benefits, the level that could and should be drawn, and whether any HMRC LTA protection is available to you, particularly in the lead up to retirement.

Getting it right now

You can see from the above that planning to draw the benefits from your accumulated retirement savings can be a complicated subject. This does not lessen the importance of the life junction that is retirement. Getting it right now can make the difference between the retirement you would like and the retirement you have to settle for.

The amount you receive from your pension fund or funds may be varied by any access to tax free cash. We will look at what you might want to think about for this in the next chapter, as another item on the menu of decisions you will need to make.

If you think about the last time you booked to go out for dinner or lunch, you made choices. You selected a restaurant or café and the time of arrival. You selected your mode of transport, perhaps car or train. You selected your table and looked through the menu to make choices as to what to eat and drink. Each choice bespoke to your preferences and requirements. A similar range of choices can occur when drawing your pension benefits, again to meet your individual needs and requirements.

Think hard about what you would like to achieve with your pension money, and what advice you may need to make the most of it.

Your nudge notes:

Your thoughts and views

- What has this chapter revealed to you about the possible ways you might want to access your pension funds? Why?

- Which pension options are attractive and why? Have you factored in the other sources of income from other assets that may be available?

- Have you thought about your dependants and the way you might want to protect them in your retirement, if at all?

- Are there challenges to the way you thought your money might work when you start to draw benefits and what are they?

- Are you going to take advice or guidance for your individual needs before you access your funds? What, if anything is going to stop you?

- Write one action that you will now implement.

6. Show me more money!

The majority of those coming into retirement may well have straightforward arrangements for their retirement income planning. A pension or two from their work over the decades, a home which might be largely mortgage free, and some accumulated savings, perhaps with the outside chance of a future inheritance, if not gobbled up by care costs. This position might have been achieved in part by the tax-free cash released when drawing pension benefits. The State Pension will be kicking in from 67 years old or so, and there are no plans for a massive spending spree when they finally stop work, other than a big holiday and possibly a kitchen or bathroom makeover. A good place to be, and still great fun to be had in the active years.

One 'problem' that might have arisen is what to do with the cash that has been released from your pension and you might well want to build this into your overall financial planning.

What to do with pension tax free cash?

The first answer to this question is anything you want to! It's your money, so you choose. The usual advantage of taking pension tax free cash is because it is tax free.

Of course, guidance and advice can help in pointing to the options that you could consider as part of your wider financial planning for the short, medium and long term. If you take pension tax free cash, invariably the taxable pension you receive will reduce to reflect the tax-free cash taken. There are always exceptions to this, with some, usually public sector, employer pensions offering a pension and cash. Please do check the details in your circumstances and seek advice where required.

I have already noted in chapter 4 the initial financial 'hygiene' plans that you might want to consider for retirement, such as maintaining a suitable level of emergency savings and reducing or paying off debt. You may plan at this life junction to make gifts to family members, as we will detail later in chapter 10.

It is also important to remember that funds held in a pension usually fall outside your estate for inheritance tax purposes. So, if you take tax free cash, you are bringing these funds inside your estate and if you are concerned about inheritance tax, this may be a factor to check.

Once any cash release you plan is achieved, if that's your choice, and perhaps some money has been spent on enjoyment, renewal of cars and home renovations, what else might you think about? When investing tax free cash, there is a range of options to look at.

This is not an exhaustive list, but you might look at the following as examples:

- The investment risk to your money might be high on the agenda, along with any ethical or environmental factors you want to take into account. There are many helpful guides which detail investment risk to help you understand and clarify your attitude to taking investment risk and your capacity for bearing any losses.

- How much cash you have in total and its allocation. You might want a percentage invested in low risk funds for a set purpose, another amount at a different risk level for a different time span, and another amount for the longer term. Have this division ready in your mind.

- Is your investment focus for income, or capital growth, or perhaps a bit of both?

- How long can you tie the money up for? The shorter the time, perhaps the lower the investment risk, especially if you have a set purpose for what you want to spend the money on.

- The tax wrapper or wrappers you use. This is where advice and guidance can help in picking out investment options that might keep any tax take from the Chancellor to a minimum. Most people in the UK have a range of annual tax allowances available to them, such as ISAs (which is a tax wrapper) that can offer a shield against tax on capital gains and income.

- How are you going to make and implement your choices? You might use a suitably qualified adviser who is likely to charge a fee, or invest directly with a provider, noting there may well still be charges that might be paid initially, or during the time your money is invested, or both. Indeed, look out for exit or early surrender charges if applicable.

- Just as a warning, there are strict rules and limits on the recycling of tax-free cash from a pension back into a pension. HMRC has been watching out for this for years.

This is just a short list of what you might need to consider when making investments from your own funds, whether they have been released from pension tax free cash or from an alternative source, such as an inheritance.

Of course, the way you accumulate cash may well vary, dependent on your personal journey, as we shall see in the next few pages. If you are not a business owner or manager, you might want to skip the balance of this chapter.

A different journey / Business owners & managers

There are those who have had a different journey to retirement, such as business owners, and the self-employed, who may have accumulated larger value assets to form the real capital value of their future income. I am referring to business assets for these individuals. These might be tangible assets, such as land, property, or machinery, or less tangible assets, such as business goodwill, client banks, intellectual property and recurring revenue streams. These may be sold as a collective, such as the assets of a whole business, perhaps the sale of a limited company, or stripped as individual assets to be sold separately. Extracting the real value is key; however, get advice on the tax treatments for each route before proceeding.

I believe that many business owners are underpaid on an annual basis for the work and risks that they take, on the understanding that the real reward for their work will come when the business is sold, merged, or transferred on. I will look at some of the aspects of these positions below.

But how do you sell a business, or its assets? You might get a direct approach, but understanding your market and who's acquiring whom, and for what purpose, is always worthwhile noting, both for information and for trends. Some business sectors become attractive to buyers over time, and you might want to choose your timing when your sector is booming.

You can use a business broker as one option, although this might be expensive. You can carefully 'let it be known' to your contacts, even your competitors, that you might be available to be acquired, or you might advertise that you are open to tenders to purchase. A quiet coffee or lunch somewhere to discuss options and open possible negotiations with a potential buyer might be the best hour or so of your time that you have ever spent. Invariably, there is no one right answer, and talking to your accountant or business adviser about options might be a good starting point.

The business sale

A business sale takes time. It will also take energy and acumen to get any deal over the line, so be ready to add this into your planning, particularly for time scales. You are likely to be selling your 'business baby', so be prepared for a somewhat emotional ride, irrespective of what any TV business boss may suggest.

And remember, selling a business may well not mean the end of your current role. It just might be the end of your work as you know it. You may be maintained as a consultant or on an 'earn out' basis for a year, or three, before you finally stop. If you expect to be on a beach sunning yourself full-time by 60, you might need to get your skates on by age 55 or so.

Selling a business can be a real can of worms for the seller, and indeed the purchaser, throughout and after the process, from the initial discussions to the Heads of Terms and sale, and any agreed targets post sale.

Advisers

It is usually important that you get your business's advisers, such as your accountant and solicitors, on board early with any approach or tender for sale to ensure they are ready to act if a suitable acquirer were to take an interest and start negotiations.

One of the key points in the paragraph above is that of finding a suitable purchaser. Your business may well have been your sole focus for a long time, and you are likely to have built up significant goodwill. It may not be particularly hard to find a purchaser, but you're not looking for 'just anybody'. There usually has to be a synergy between the buyer and seller that outside contacts and suppliers can recognise and with whom they are comfortable to continue trading. You do not want to create a rod for your own back in selling to an organisation that does not share any of your business ethics or business culture, especially if the sale price offered is on a phased payment basis, dependent on targeted future performance.

Initial documents

You are likely to need to sign a non-disclosure document for any future potential sale in advance of negotiations, and your solicitor or legal adviser may want to vet this first before you proceed. Please do engage with them at an early stage of the process.

Initial negotiations are likely, if agreed, to lead to a Heads of Terms document, which each party holds, usually along with their legal advisers, to detail what sale headlines have been agreed as a way forward in securing the deal once all due diligence is complete and all parties are satisfied. These Heads of Terms documents are not normally legally binding, unless specified, so speak to your solicitors to know where you are.

Due diligence

Due diligence is the process through which a purchaser would usually have unfettered access to your accounts, documents, systems and processes, both now and over past business years. It's like a full service and MOT of your business 'engine' to check what is being purchased is actually what is being sold. Be ready, because there are likely to be a lot of intrusive questions on many aspects of your business.

What would you pick out from your business that needs polishing up to make sure it would pass scrutiny? And you will know the issues within your business better than anyone. It might be worth addressing these points now, because self-scrutiny is better than external scrutiny if your record keeping is not quite as thorough as you would like. When is the last time that you reviewed your cost control and the regular invoices that you pay to see what value they really offer? Perhaps some cost cutting to improve profitability might be well worthwhile before you start your sale process.

Timing

Rarely in our experience is a sale achieved in a short period of time, such as three to six months. You might want to anticipate a year's period to get any sale completed, noting that, subject to your agreement, there may be an earn out period (during which the seller 'earns' part of the sale price, based on performance), say 12-24 months, or a handover period, say 6-12 months. Invariably, the sale price might reflect the smooth transition of assets, orders, work in progress and team members. I have only seen one business sold to a competitor with the process from start to finish completing in about three months, with no ongoing liability or tie-in. They do happen, but they are rare!

Plan ahead and speak to your accountant about what your position might be, and how you might start the process of letting it be known that you are on the market for a suitor. Ask them about their experiences to gain a greater depth of understanding.

Name your price?

What would you pay for your business today? If a fellow business owner or a competitor was in your premises today, and got out their cheque book and asked you to name your price, what would it be? This is a reasonable possibility, and you need to be ready to answer.

A fair follow-up question might be how you got to that number. You need to be confident that you know what you are talking about and why you want a specified amount.

There are a few accounting methods to calculate a business's value, often involving a multiple of annual income, and quite likely dependent on the recurrence of the annual income stream. You'll probably hear the term 'EBITDA' bandied about pretty early on in the negotiations. This stands for 'earnings before interest, taxes, depreciation and amortisation', and is one measure of a company's overall financial performance. It can be used as an alternative to net income, although the most appropriate measure of your business's value will depend on the industry or profession you're in and the nature of your business.

Payment structure

Based on current tax legislation, which can and does change, you may well be entitled to Business Asset Disposal Relief on the sale proceeds of your business assets. This used to be known as Entrepreneurs' Relief. This might reduce the capital gains tax that you might ordinarily suffer on the sale of business assets. Your accountant should be able to help you with this, but do take care. Tax might be due on completion, even if the sale proceeds are spread over a few years, so make sure you know where you stand. You don't want to have to return your dream car or house because the tax came up early to bite you!

The sale proceeds might be paid at the sale date, or in part payments, or in cash and purchaser shares. This will depend on what you negotiate and may help or hamper your needs for immediate cash on the sale of a company.

Other points and issues

Commercial property sale (owned directly or via a pension, or both)

One possible benefit of property ownership, either commercial or residential, is that it is tangible. You can drive past it, touch it and see its physical form. And the property might be owned by you directly, by your business, by your pension fund, or by a combination of the above.

One key disadvantage of property is that it could take a good period of time to sell it if you needed to move quickly, whilst getting a fair price. This will need to be factored into your planning if you need to raise funds from the sale for your retirement plans. I understand that there are lots of tax variables for property, so take a look at what can be achieved.

Some commercial properties are owned by pension funds maintained by the business owner and let to the company being sold. If a new business owner is taking over a lease granted by your pension on the sale of your business, you will need to be confident that the new owner has the plans and cashflow to maintain the rental income to your business in the longer term, especially if you plan to rely on it as a pension income source.

Other investment sales

Like property and business assets, some investment assets can take time to sell. If you have unusual assets that you plan to sell to meet your retirement capital and income needs, then please leave enough time to get these sold and the money banked, after any tax is due. You do not want to be in a 'fire-sale' if you have to sell quickly in a poor market.

Much to consider

There is much to consider in this chapter. With your retirement planning underway, what will you do with any cash that is made available to you, either from a pension, or from an inheritance, or business sale? Don't forget to factor in some fun. And you might well need a break after going through the process of selling your business.

Thinking again about the process of selling a business, I think the key question and point is being able to name your price, month in, month out. It is not uncommon for a good business to be approached on a regular basis about selling. If you know your price and are able to indicate this to any potential purchaser, it will sort the wheat of those who are really serious from the chaff of those who will waste your time. There are many time-stealers out there, so be careful!

If you are a business owner starting your retirement process, then take a long hard look at your business to see if you would buy it, good points and problems combined. If you can engineer out those problems now, and over the next few years to increase the sale price value, what's stopping you?

Your nudge notes:

Your thoughts and views

- Are you going to take pension tax free cash, and if you are, what are you going to do with it?

- What's the main issue with any business you own/run? Why? And how are you going to repair/improve/enhance it soon?

- What challenges do you face to selling your business or business assets to match the timing of your retirement? Would you buy your business?

- How will you engage with your business advisers to help you achieve positive outcomes? Are you ready to sell? Have you left enough time?

- Write one action that you, or your adviser, will now implement.

7. Last chance to make your retirement comfortable

You've probably worked hard to get to where you are, and the dash to the finish line is not over yet. The last few years of your working career are the times that will really count towards maximising all that you can, both mentally and financially.

You may well have reached your most senior position, be earning at a reasonable level, and have excess funds that could be channelled towards retirement assets to use in a few years' time. It's never normally too late to save.

It's taken you significant energy, time, experience, tenacity, and wisdom to make it all happen, indeed a working lifetime! And remember, the income levels that you are achieving now may never be repeatable. Be careful of wishing your work life away to retire, because if your post retirement income doesn't stack up when you have stopped, the chances of your returning to those past earnings might be slim. So, take this last period of work to fill your boots whilst you are able, and have the energy to do so.

We have had many conversations with those who would stop work in a heartbeat, given a chance, because they dislike the hours, the stress, the commute, the people, the boss, the industry...you get the idea. If you can afford to retire, and it's the right decision for you, then fine. However, if you can focus for an extra period of work, say two years as an example, it can make all the difference to the funds and cash available for your retirement. Many believe, often incorrectly, that their money will last longer than their life. They may realise their error when it's too late, noting the Office for National Statistics report on the significant numbers now living to age 85 plus (around 1.67M in the UK in mid-2020 – source: ONS).

Financial transition

If you think that you are an expert on retirement savings, having looked at length into the world of retirement, then please be careful. There are usually many ways that varying types of pension plan can be used, or flexed, to get a bit more out of them. We are not damning with faint praise those who think they know it all. Quite the contrary. Checking in with an adviser even just to clarify your thinking may well throw up a different way of achieving a better overall financial position.

Some struggle to keep working and if you are fighting for tangible motivation, buy yourself a large calendar and cross out each day as it is completed, with a highlight marked at a future date when you will finally stop. It may not add real value, but it will give a readily focused routine which will literally see the days tick by. This works for some, but not all. How are you going to make it to the planned end date?

For a start, it can really help to understand the real benefit that continuing to work will give you in retirement. You're not only continuing to earn, which defers the need to draw on your pensions and accumulated capital, you are also usually building up additional pension and other savings for your future. The combined effect can be surprisingly powerful, and hopefully a good motivator to keep you going. This is something we regularly quantify and model for our fifty-something clients, both as an argument for continuing to work for a little longer and as a predictor for the optimum time to stop.

Let's look at some of the parameters that you may consider, or that may occur, in the last few years of work as you reach your destination.

Do you spend all of your income now?

When working, many people budget to meet their household costs and liabilities as they arise. Whether this is salary or dividends or a combination of both, the money flows in each month, and then, sadly, out again to pay the bills.

Thinking about your current position, do you use all your income now? And if you move into retirement, either in full or on a phased basis, will the savings and pension benefits you have currently accrued allow you to continue on without making changes to your annual or monthly budget, or lifestyle?

You should be able to take some cost savings into account in this calculation – commuting costs will reduce or cease when you stop work or reduce your hours, and then there's the deductions from your pay to consider, such as pension contributions, National Insurance and so on. Plus the daily sandwich, coffee, drinks after work...although these costs may well be replaced with other social activities in retirement.

Lost work benefits? The less obvious points

When you think about the benefits package that you receive through your current role, you might include salary, car and pension, or dividends and drawings if you are a business owner or self-employed.

As an employee, and as an example, you may have also enjoyed other protection benefits, such as death in service cover, perhaps three or four times your salary, along with income protection in the event of your long-term ill health, and private medical insurance, sometimes known as PMI. The value of each benefit to you will be personal to your circumstances, but each needs to be considered in your future planning to see if you want to replicate, or indeed continue cover, where possible, when your work comes to an end. Some employers' private medical insurance schemes will allow you to carry on cover into retirement as an example, normally without the re-imposition of any new joiner restrictions. Check the premium costs for you first to make sure these meet with your budget.

This might be important if you are currently claiming or have recently made a medical claim or want to continue to protect family members. Whilst paid by the employer, this type of cover is a taxable benefit in kind. However, this position ends when you pay the premiums directly.

You might also lose a company car or computer that you use, and the cost of replacing these may need to be built into your capital needs when making any transition from work to retirement.

Can't be bothered to collect free money?

For those who are working longer and joining a new employer later in their lives, invariably they will be joined into the employer's pension scheme. This was mandated by law some years back and requires a pension contribution from the member, but importantly also from the employer, unless you opt out. The member's pension contribution will also attract some tax relief, so the government to a lesser extent chips into this new pension pot. Free money! What a lovely thought and where can I sign?

We have on many an occasion heard the comments, 'not going to work for long, so can't be bothered' or 'not sure it's worth the effort for such small amounts of money' from those who plan only to work for a further year or two. An individual can opt out, but unless they have a very big pension already accrued, or have some restrictions on pensions, joining is usually worthwhile, even for short periods, to pick up the employer contribution.

If you saw a twenty-pound note unclaimed on the floor, you probably wouldn't hesitate to pick it up. These pension plans are also free money from an employer. All you have to do is join in and contribute and the employer will do the rest. Extracting value where you can, especially if your pension benefits may not be as you would want them, is important at every opportunity, and an offer from an employer to add to your pension is not normally one to be missed.

From the minimum retirement age, currently 55, you can get your funds back through tax free cash to 25% as a standard and the balance as taxable income, with the tax being based on your overall income in the tax year you take it. Even with tax taken, you should be better off because of the additional contributions from the government and your old boss, although this will also depend on other factors, such as where your fund was invested and how it performed over time. You will know by now that past performance is not a guarantee of future performance and that fund values in personal pensions can fall as well as rise. You have been warned.

Easy to forget an old pension policy here or there

The likelihood of an individual aged 50 or so having accumulated three or four workplaces over the thirty-ish years that they have been working is not uncommon. Conversely, having just one employer over your working life is now unusual.

You can probably guess that it is easy to lose contact with an old employer, and importantly the pension that might have accumulated whilst working and which has been deferred since leaving. You might have a number of separate pensions accumulated as you start to look at your retirement plans. What do they all mean?

Some people have a full understanding of what pension benefit is held where, and some don't. If you have lost contact with an old employer's pension plan, or indeed a personal arrangement (do you remember the scramble in 1988 to contract out of the State Earnings Related Pension Scheme (SERPS) to a private pension under a Thatcher pension initiative?), you can check online. There are no-cost, government-provided ways of tracing these older plans, noting that many insurance companies have merged into each other or changed name. Some benefits may have been transferred into a single pot, which some investors prefer.

We suggest that you have a look back at your employment history to identify employers and their pensions, if you were a member, to ensure nothing is missing. If you suspect there is, you might want to write to them now to give them a wake-up call to say you are still alive, still own the deferred benefit, and will want an update of value. Some older schemes might be a defined benefit/final salary type plan, and these can have significant guarantees and benefits within them, although it may not appear so from the somewhat confusing statements that you may receive.

Checking to see what's where regarding your pension benefits, and with which providers, is well worthwhile throughout your working life, if only to keep them updated with any address changes so that you do not become orphaned from their database. It's not difficult for this to happen, to the extent that a group of pension providers launched the UK's first National Pension Tracing Day on 31 October 2021. The initiative noted that at that point, there was around £19.4 billion in unclaimed pension pots (Source: nationalpensiontracingday.co.uk).

Through our work with clients approaching retirement, we regularly identify lost pension plans from previous employment, some with significant benefits that add real value to an individual's pension and tax-free cash position. Communicating the good news to a surprised and happy client is one of the most gratifying aspects of our work.

Multiple sources of income

You might have enjoyed one source of income through your working life. This might have been through payroll, or through your own company or business.

The situation may well change in retirement with a range of incomes being paid, for varying amounts and on different timescales.

In retirement, you might receive a pension paid monthly, along with a State Pension, which is currently paid every four weeks. If pension income is paid from an income drawdown arrangement, you may want to vary income over time, and this is usually achievable. You may also have some consultancy work, or part-time income during your transition from work to full retirement.

In addition, you may also have investment or rental income from other arrangements such as an ISA, an investment portfolio, or buy-to-let property. Each may pay different income amounts at different times, with some income being taxable, and other income, such as from an ISA, being paid tax free. A good example might be dividend income from an investment portfolio. Dividend income will normally be 'lumpy' over a calendar or tax year, with income in some periods being higher than in others, dependent on the individual holdings, how much they pay out and the frequency of these payments. These possible income variances need to be anticipated and managed from a personal cash-flow perspective.

Over the year, it may be a combination of income streams that help you to reach your target income in retirement. It might be a bit cumbersome administratively, so be ready for any tax return you need to complete. Each source of taxable income will need to be taken into account for income tax purposes, and it is worth noting that most pensions are paid with the deduction of income tax already accounted for. HMRC issues a tax code to the pension provider before a payment is made. If a code is not available, it is likely that the pension provider will pay the income after the deduction of emergency tax, and this can then be adjusted later on. You may want to seek tax advice from a suitably qualified adviser, such as an accountant, if required.

You can see from the notes above that having three or more sources of income in retirement as your overall 'pension' is not uncommon for retirees.

Taking value from your State Pension and longevity

It is currently planned that the State Pension age will increase in future years based on perceived increasing average longevity. For a 55-year-old, the current minimum age to draw will be 67. However, this does not mean that you as an individual will live any longer. The State Pension is an unfunded pension arrangement, paying out to pensioners from the funds brought in by those currently working and making National Insurance contributions. With average longevity across the UK (lower ages in some areas of the UK, and higher in other areas) being around 82 as a rough example, and with the State Pension age rising to 67 and possibly age 68 after a planned review for those of us aged around 50, the average payment term might only be 15 years or so. If you are not average and you don't make it, you might not have gained value, and if you live to 90, you are 'quids in', as they say. Is it worth deferring, allowing benefits in deferment to increase over time, noting that the benefit is liable to income tax? You decide, but be careful not to stack the longevity odds against yourself.

Gap year(s) of income

For some who are now in their mid-fifties, the opportunity to take a gap year before starting university or work was not an option. Indeed, I am not sure that it ever really reared its head on the options list of life when I finished my A-level studies. Work beckoned, well a salary did anyway!

Roll forward thirty-five plus years and, ironically, gap years may reappear on the curriculum of life, but this time from an income perspective, rather than having a year backpacking round Europe.

Some decide that they will stop work at an age to suit them, which might be before deferred pension benefits or State Pension income becomes available. They move from a regular income to no income. They have a range of pension assets that could be accessed, but sometimes not without significant penalties for drawing early. These can be financially painful to the member, and this is often the case with defined benefit/final salary type plans.

The security that a final salary type pension scheme normally offers means that concerns about investment markets should not affect the guaranteed income you receive. When in payment, the pension may well increase with inflation in whole or in part, and you should keep an eye on this. If inflation is high and your pension increases are not, the income you have may not keep pace with rising costs and maintain real purchasing power.

Many final salary plans are now closed to new joiners and to continued accrual from existing members, with employers moving their employees to personal pension type plans, for

116

instance, which are generally lower cost and lower risk to the company. These personal pension plans can offer greater flexibility in the way funds can be accessed, as an example using an income drawdown plan.

If there are gap years in income between employment and reaching State Pension age, or the age at which other pension plans can be drawn with nil or minimum penalty, these personal pension plans can be a source to fill in the income gap period. It might fairly be argued that the income and tax-free cash from the personal pension plan could be subsidising the reduction in penalty from the other deferred pension(s). It's certainly an option worth checking.

This opportunity, if it is one available to you, needs to be investigated carefully as part of your overall retirement income planning, both for now and in the decades ahead.

Death nominations on your pension

This is an important note.

When you are in contact with a pension provider, check the nomination on any fund that you hold to ensure any death benefits available under the plan are nominated in the way you want. It is not uncommon to find an old pension nominated to an ex-spouse, old boyfriend or girlfriend or in one memorable experience, a mistress. There were some red faces in that meeting!

Check your money documents, even in retirement

I have had the honour of commenting on BBC local radio for over fifteen years, talking about many money related subjects.

I usually prepare some notes to help both me and the DJ through what can be pretty dry topics. Making money planning interesting, or at least of some appeal to a wide audience, can be tricky at times, but this does not change its importance.

Often, for those less motivated by money planning, I have advocated that if they check one thing regularly, make it your payslip or your annual pension statement. For the payslip, it's good to know what's being paid and what's being deducted. Most importantly, you want to know how much you're actually going to get.

If you are getting a pension or you're in employment, you are also likely to get an annual P60 tax form, and this can be a helpful way of checking that any income tax deducted at source is correct. If not, you might need to pay more, or seek a refund. Don't be fooled by well-meaning suggestions to avoid HMRC at all costs. They are normally very friendly and certainly there to help you. Engage with them if need be, to get your income tax right.

In the same way, have a look at your annual pension statement if you're getting pension income, or if you plan to at a later date. Have a look at any deductions, such as costs and charges, perhaps the performance of the fund or the health of the pension scheme against its liabilities to make sure that all seems correct.

If you're not sure, then have a look at last year's statement to compare or speak to your financial adviser if you have one to get their professional view. We know that this might not be the most exciting of exercises, but a check or two should add peace of mind, which is always worth it.

Small funds matter

As an additional note in this regard: if your pension fund is small, please don't think that it is not important. A pound is a pound in anyone's hands. Some financial advice companies will only engage with fund values in the hundreds of thousands. If you don't fit that mould, then research your locality to see who can help. There will be someone who can give you good advice and guidance. There are a few government agencies that can also help to signpost your options at no cost, and this might also be a useful way to gather your thinking together.

Your nudge notes:

**Coming in to Land – Runway to Retirement
Chapter 7: Last chance to make your retirement
comfortable**

Your thoughts and views

- **Your runway landing is ahead! What will you do now to make it the destination of your choice?**

- **Do you spend all your income now? When's the last time you looked at income and outgoings to see if you could achieve greater efficiency with your money?**

- **Have you thought back to your employment past to see if there are any missing pensions that might not be gathered in? Can you check?**

- When is the last time you checked your financial documents to see all seems to be correct? If not recently, take the time to do this now.

- Are you likely to have 'income gap years' between stopping work and drawing other pension benefits? Have you thought through how these can be 'filled' efficiently?

- Write one action that you will now implement.

8. Never going to retire...and alternatives

There are those who hope that buying a lottery ticket regularly will resolve their retirement conundrum and provide a financial security backstop in their old age, whilst not making many other plans. Perhaps not the best of financial strategies. If they had put their lottery ticket money into a pension, they might have seen a greater return.

The reality is that many find their work tedious, repetitive and dull, week in, week out. They are just trying to survive, but not yet ready to throw in the towel. If you fall into this category and you think about your work now, if you could change one thing, what would it be? You probably have the answer already, and if you know what it is, have you asked your employer about making a change? As long as it is reasonable, put a suggestion forward to see if it will help both you and others.

There are also those who are fully focused on all things retirement and will be out of the door on the date they have had planned for years, as we have witnessed.

Another group of individuals swears that they will never retire and curses the thought of ending work. I think my wife fears this of me because I enjoy what I do.

Mark Twain is credited with saying, "Find a job you enjoy doing, and you will never have to work a day in your life." Very true.

Some fear that they would 'go mad' if they did not have something to do, or to tinker with, regardless of their financial situation. Pottering around in a shed or greenhouse at the bottom of the garden fulfils many a retiree. Do you see this for yourself, or have you something more in mind?

Then there are those who just ignore any retirement thoughts because they never plan to make it that far, and when they actually do, they'll have to keep going.

Some people have simply not planned ahead for retirement. This might be for various reasons, not least of all money, or lack of it. They still have to pay the bills and they hope that perhaps their home or an inheritance is going to be their pension fund to see them into old age, along with the State Pension. We have seen this type of approach often, and there are risks associated with it. For some individuals, the need to keep working to bring in money is dictated by others in their lives, and this is not uncommon.

If your plan is never to retire, then your strategy and course still need to be plotted to make sure that you stick to your objectives. You may have limited choice because of limited funds, but what do you expect to happen, and will you have the physical and mental capacity to achieve your work longevity? Technology may also erode the value of the work you do, and you would not want to be replaced by a computer.

Having your head in the sand about retirement planning is one thing but taking the same stubborn stance when planning what the alternative is - continuing to work - is another thing. Don't be disappointed about your life choices: they are part of the mix that makes you unique and can guide you in your future decisions. Even if the position you find yourself in is not as positive as you might have preferred, or perhaps was a consequence of circumstances, make the best of what you have. Thinking it through step by step and taking action may well work. Dwelling on the past will only exacerbate a difficult situation: accept, move on and above all, plan. We appreciate that is easier to write than to achieve and we are not glossing over what may be troubling times. Start by achieving some control and understanding of where you are, and where you want – realistically – to be. Money may be the constraining factor and talking to friends and family may well help.

Plans versus reality?

When it comes to the crunch, although you might have planned to downsize at retirement, the thought of moving might in reality be unbearable, or maybe the kids protest the sale of the family home. Perhaps the parents that did not live 'three score years and ten' to seventy actually made it to 90, having accrued massive care home costs that consumed any inheritance that might have been expected. As a side note, the government does have plans to change how care home fees are charged, although as you can guess, the detail already reveals a few 'devils' in the way the reality of costs may roll out.

It is important to be ready for these life eventualities because they are not uncommon. Making and reviewing plans for your money and your future, hopefully as an additional strategy to the ones noted above, may add in more overall flexibility. If you don't plan, and if you do stay working, then you need to be able to accept and live with your life choices.

Older relatives and inheritance tax

This book focuses on the runway to retirement and there are other related topics, such as long-term care, that we have set aside, noting that this is for most another phase of their later life. In your mid-fifties, you may be dealing with this situation for older relatives and friends who will lean on you for help and support. The silent generation, pre-baby-boomers (1928-1945), may have accumulated significant wealth, but may have had no life experience as to how to spend their money. The money just 'happened', and they lived their lives frugally from the start. It's not uncommon to find large and forgotten savings accounts coming out of the woodwork.

One other topic that might begin to raise its head is inheritance tax, with your having accumulated some wealth over the decades of your hard work. In most cases, pension assets fall outside your estate for inheritance tax purposes, based on current legislation, and can be a good source of protection for an estate in the event of death. You may want to check and take advice for your own arrangements to ensure that all the documentation you have is pointing in the right direction and is as efficient as you would want for your loved ones.

What will tip you over the edge?

Some combinations are all positive. Eric and Ernie, Ant and Dec, surf and turf, drum and bass to name a random few (hopefully we have covered a range of ages in that list!).

The factors that bring an individual to the point of retiring may be a combination of events, emotions, and rule changes that makes you feel, no, I'm not doing this anymore, it's not worth it. It's rarely one thing. The rule from years ago that you had to stop work when you reached the normal retirement age set out in your employment contract has long gone; however, it does still provide some framework for individuals to consider their options.

Your combination might be a war of attrition at work, such as the loss of business due to COVID, a new lease to be signed, or a regulatory change with associated costs that brings you to the conclusion that work must end. Perhaps a new boss or line manager, a change in employment contract terms, or an effective (and demoralising) demotion through a corporate restructure. The regulatory rule changes in the financial services sector are so regular, and often have the feeling of a sledgehammer to crack a nut, that I think it will be this area that will finally get us.

Or perhaps, and this is a key point for many, the effects of the pandemic and our emergence from the period has made you re-assess your lifestyle and working life and has brought what is important into clear perspective. The exodus from cities to more rural locations provides evidence of many thousands of people's desires to be away from the rat race and commutes. With mobile connectivity so readily available, this is an option that could never have been achieved a decade ago. Will the rural idyll wane and a return to the cities begin? Recent statistics suggest that this might be the case.

There might be more positive reasons in your combination, such as grandchildren arriving and the opportunity to help that may attract you away from work. The chance to buy a boat, or a home abroad, or simply a house move and integration into a new community, or a dog for company and exercise might just push you over the emotional edge. And remember, big decisions take time, because rarely does an individual head back to work once they are made.

The reality is that it is likely to be an emotional combination, both good and bad, that will give you that 'eureka' moment of knowing you are finally going to stop work and retire. Something just clicks.

It is only then that you will truly own your decision to retire. Take responsibility and enjoy it. I hope that day is liberating in many ways.

Consequences of keeping going & alternatives

Work in its varying formats can have consequences, usually focused on age, ability, agility and wellbeing.

Sports people may physically not be able to continue at the highest levels of competition after a certain age, perhaps ages 35-45. Some take time to acquire the depth of knowledge within a profession to be able to undertake the work that they do. Alternatively, some careers and professions lend themselves to not retiring. Indeed, many individuals after their first retirement and chosen path, re-invent themselves to start a second career, either paid or otherwise.

Charitable and community works

Working within the community, a good cause, higher education, perhaps completing that degree that always eluded them due to time constraints, or charity work is very common as people aim to use their acquired skills and acumen to add value where they can.

We know a man who retired from his work as a sales director at age 65, started his own company as a second career in the same industry, and then, as a third career, retrained as an electrician. He's still working now at age eighty-something and enjoying it.

However, keep a look out for those who will take advantage of your newfound enthusiasm, because you might utter the words, 'I don't know why I bothered' before too long, contrary to all that you had anticipated. The same eighty-something chap mentioned above had some challenging experiences with business partners in the organisation, hence the complete switch to electrical work, which he now loves.

As a key positive, be clear to yourself about what you want to put in, what others are expecting of you, and what and when you want to get out to avoid any unexpected disappointments. There are limits and you need to note these. I once joined the board of a charity and the first thing I did was to give notice that I would be resigning in six years' time. This gave all involved scope to know how long my commitment and energy would last, and the target date to leave. I kept to my commitment date and maintained my momentum. Communication is key in managing expectations here.

Before you agree to join the arranging committee or board of a group, organisation or charity, have a look at the organisation's accounts and their current business plan. This is to make sure that the organisation is financially viable before you start. Also, by joining a board, you might agree to a term of three years as an example as part of their agreed rotation basis, allowing yourself to stand, or not, for re-election after that time. Some organisations may maintain other parameters, such as age limits, and you need to look out for these. You should be comfortable to commit to the service term anticipated and to have the skills that they want you for in the role that they have available.

Coaching others to progress / being a mentor

However old you are, if you are still working, or if you have retired but want to use your decades of accumulated knowledge to help others, why not consider coaching or mentoring others. This can be within your current workplace, through a charity initiative such as Young Enterprise, or through involvement with local schools, as examples. There are many more avenues. In addition, coaching and mentoring does not necessarily need to focus on your specific profession as such, although you may choose for it to do so. Remember that you will have gathered a range of workplace related skills over time, maybe from being able to read and understand company accounts to knowing how to chair a meeting professionally, and, importantly, wrap up succinctly. For younger individuals just entering the workplace, even some help on how to make an approach, and how to behave with their new colleagues might be crucial to their early success and could really build their confidence.

Technology abounds

The world has changed dramatically since you first started work. We could head off at this stage with the usual anecdotes of our school years with no mobile phones, no internet and having just about got our first neolithic computers in the classroom when we reached another phase of our lives. All walks of life have evolved with the ever-improving technology that has made us all more efficient, and this will not end. Imagine technology making us all more efficient at retirement, extracting greater fun from all that we do. Yes please!

Technology has touched and changed our lives and will continue to do so into retirement, however that looks. It should be embraced, noting of course that this can bring its frustrations, and indeed notable negatives, such as scams. Seek help from those you trust, if needed, to help keep up with the pace of technology changes.

Be comfortable with your choices

There is no right answer as to whether working, retiring or a mixture of the two is the best option for an individual. It is simply their choice, based on their own circumstances. There are alternatives outside work, such as community involvement, that can run alongside your free time or your working life. As long as you are comfortable with your decisions, that is really all that matters.

Your nudge notes:

<u>Your thoughts and views</u>

- If you think you will never retire, is this because of the fear of being bored in retirement or because of the finances, or both? What's good, bad or indifferent?

- Is your retirement hope focused on a property sale or inheritance? Is there anything more you can do now to lessen the possible risk of this not working out?

- Do you have any contingency plans to help you both emotionally and financially if you have to stop work?

• What skills do you have that you could transfer to others to help them with their careers? How will you achieve this? What's your motivation?

• Can technology help you with your future plans?

• Do you have a chosen cause or community project that you would like to get involved with when you retire? Why them and have you made contact yet?

• Write one action that you will now implement.

9. What's going to stop you?

If life was a smooth path, there would be no reason to plan ahead. However, we know that life gets in the way of all great planning. Life problems have been going on, well, for all our lives. Each one putting a swerve or twist in our plans, and as you will see, there are many serious issues that can crop up. You will need to adapt to survive!

If you have reached your State Pension age, you will also have the option to apply for a free bus pass, so not much is going to stop you now! Well, perhaps a few things might, in reality, as life is hardly ever a smooth path. If it were, though, it would probably be quite boring, and we're all used to life throwing a spanner in the works just at the wrong time to bring challenges, rewards and sometimes unwanted excitement. You might have become a master at juggling the family finances and emotions to cope with the unexpected during your current working life. We can assure you that life in retirement will at points be just as challenging by not following the path you anticipated.

Some people feel that they have had enough and that it's time to make real positive changes, and not return to pre-COVID life. As an example, the Bloomberg news website reported in October 2021 an estimate of over three million Americans retiring early because of the crisis (source: Bloomberg)

Closer to home, in March 2021, the insurance company Legal & General reported on research it had carried out, noting that some 1.3 million people planned to retire early due to the pandemic (source: Legal & General).

In contrast, others feel that the crisis set their retirement plans back by some years: as an example, the Legal & General research from March 2021 notes that around 1.45 million people planned to delay retirement by over three years on average.

Which are you, and have your retirement date plans stayed intact, irrespective of the pandemic? If things have changed, you were not alone in fighting to keep your head above water as you faced some unwelcome, or welcome outcomes and financial effects experienced both nationally and globally over the difficult period.

In this chapter, I have added some of the possible life issues that might crop up, and some will be of no surprise. I have aimed to try and 'cage' these life points in one chapter, so that you can dip into this section as you see fit. Bite-sized chunks if you like, perhaps as a test of your own plans.

Some might suggest that the points below are not 'negatives', simply some realism, and that's fine. Life happens, but it is the way that you deal with it that matters, and your emotions will play a key part in all that you achieve. These emotions will have been carved from the rock that is you and are the collective of your experiences. Remember, proof is personal!

Fear

Fear is a hugely powerful emotion. It can be used against an individual, group or society to control its very being. We have witnessed the fear created by the pandemic and its risks to health, and how controlling this can be, either by mandate from the authorities, or personally by the way we have curtailed our activities over those years.

Fear can also be a factor in the way you plan your retirement and particularly your money. Will you have enough money to see you through your life – or, conversely, will you have enough life over which to spend your money? The latter is quite often the case for the wealthy: you only have to look at the current rise in the inheritance tax take by the Treasury for proof. Having enough to repay a mortgage or sufficient equity to downsize to live debt free, or releasing property equity by other means to spend. To have some emergency savings, and enough income to treat the grandchildren at birthdays or Christmas are all reasonable expectations.

Loneliness and depression

It's a big wrench to leave work, even if it was your choice. The structure, colleague interaction, chat and camaraderie may be all gone, perhaps with a final trip to the pub and a goodbye present now sat on your mantlepiece. Thanks for all the memories and cheerio!

The end of work can be depressing for some and recognising and planning for these real personal risks early is all important.

If leaving work is down to you, rather than forced upon you for some reason, you will have some idea at least of when you intend to go, even if it's just a vague understanding of the length of your notice period. This means that you will know what season you will retire into, and we often suggest spring or summer if there is a choice, as it means that you will start your retirement in decent weather, with a range of outdoor activity options, rather than in the gloomy and cold winter months. It might sound a bit trivial, but the weather when you retire really will make a difference to what you choose to do.

If you know whether you're likely to be facing rain or shine when work ends, you can start to plan some activities, whether these are entirely new, or focused on existing hobbies and interests. As noted earlier in this book, if you have been able to plan your leaving date, you will also have time to investigate who might be doing, or already have done, the same thing, so that you have like-minded people to meet up with and enjoy time together when work ends. We will add more thoughts to this topic in the next chapter.

Whatever you enjoy, the key point is to plan in things to look forward to, activities you enjoy and a good amount of social interaction. It is very easy to let the social aspect of life slip if the main way in which you achieved this in the past was through work. Loneliness has been proven to be dangerous and is very much to be avoided if at all possible.

If you don't have a choice about when you leave work, this still stands. You might not have as much notice to decide what retirement will look like, but you can still ensure that your days are fulfilling and active. It might take you a little longer to decide what 'fulfilment' means to you, but you will get there.

Physical and mental health

I have suggested in this book that time is most valuable, even more than money. Perhaps I am wrong because health has to be as important as both these commodities. Without good health, we may be limited as to what we can achieve.

A local business contact suggested that being over age 50 had its inspirations, namely a new and interesting ache or pain every day. They weren't wrong as I can personally testify: some musculo-skeletal deterioration is, sadly, inevitable as you age. So much to look forward to!

A major catalyst for one couple's decision to retire was, sadly, the husband suffering a major heart attack at home. Work had been stressful and constant, and his enjoyment of fine food, wine and cigars caught up with him one afternoon when alone in the house. He remembers talking to the emergency services on the home phone as he slipped in and out of consciousness, and he also remembers worrying that he had to have his mobile and wallet in clear view if he died to ensure that his loved ones knew where they were. He was blue-lighted to hospital and a few days in intensive care followed.

He and his wife had already been thinking about what retirement might look like, and this event clarified their view that they needed to act in bringing their business interests to a close. The husband suffered another heart attack a few months later, minor this time, and this was the final point that made them ask the retirement pilot to bring them into land promptly, rather than continuing to circle for a landing slot.

The wonders of medical science had controlled the situation and restored past health as much as possible. They sold up their home, bought a dog, changed the cars, and relocated away from the ever-increasing traffic and commute times. Their new location, some 100 miles away from their old life, had been selected because they had a few friends there and it was where a grandfather had once lived. Their knowledge of the area was historic and suited their planned new lifestyle.

I met them in their mid-transition process and they were happy with the choices they had made that far, although their objectives had adjusted since first being set. The original path they had set was not without its challenges, with a new home renovation and some work commitments to tie up. However, one additional key observation for her was that they were young enough to make the transition, both being around 62/63 years old.

Cheating yourself?

As another observation, I spoke to an old friend one afternoon about her views of the future. She is about five years older than me and made a few interesting observations. She confirmed that 'we are the make-up of the parts of our past' and commented on how different we all are because of this. Her view at the end of the conversation was that the first phase of retirement, the active years, might last to age 75, and that if work didn't end until 65 or 67, or even later, then you were cheating yourself out of these valuable active years. Leave it too long and you might manage a bit of fun, but would soon be moving into potentially the less active years of the second phase of retirement, which we have termed the fulfilled years.

She also suggested, and I had not heard this for a good few years, that she 'did not want to be the richest person in the graveyard!'. There is some mileage in this statement, noting of course that many underestimate how long they will live, given the wonders of modern medical science. The costs of long-term care is certainly one issue for many that might ensure that this fear of dying rich does not actually happen in reality.

Old ailments

You might have been born with ailments that have been resolved or controlled over your life so far. However, their consequences may come to haunt you in later life. Just ask my ever-aching hip (yes, the supposedly good one, ironically) how it's coping, and you might guess the answer. So, for me, future mobility is a factor as to perhaps where I live in terms of location, and certainly a point of note when considering the type of property I may purchase in the future. It should be noted that many families have inherited health traits, such as high blood pressure, high cholesterol, or alternatively extended longevity. These points and factors should be considered in the overall picture of yourself and your health.

Mental health and wellbeing is as important as physical wellbeing. You may well have enjoyed, or indeed endured, a regimented work routine all your working life. The humdrum of the 9-5 routine can be seen as a curse but provides a structure that can be relied upon. It may well be hard to break away from such a virtual shackle, especially if it happens abruptly, such as through redundancy.

What to do?

From a basic health point of view, when's the last time you had a medical check-up? If it was a long time ago, then get your health checked now and make this an annual or twice-yearly routine from now on. Once a year, I have my bloods fully checked to ensure that all is functioning as it should. It doesn't help the hip situation, but hey, you can't win them all. No one can tell you how long you will live, but a regular medical might identify early any issues of note. You do not want to be a late presenter for serious health conditions, such as cancer, if you can avoid it. 'Range anxiety' is a new-ish term for electric vehicles and how long their batteries will last before you get stuck on the side of a road somewhere. Don't do the same with your health.

Of course, sadly, many people, historically men, will still stick their heads in the sand when it comes to caring for their own personal health and wellbeing. If you are one of them, please do object to this statement and prove me wrong. Get your health checked regularly.

Exercise is also a really important part of a healthy and happy retirement. I think it's a bit rich of me to advocate the virtues of exercise, but here goes! When the UK locked down in March 2020, I started the next day to use a static exercise bike to 'virtually' cycle to work. The 30-minute session in the garage each morning would see about 40 kilometres cycled per week, before returning into the house to start the working day from home. This has continued and 7000 kilometres later, along with a few press-ups, I don't believe that I have ever looked or felt fitter. This is not without its consequences (see hip above, along with other aches and pains) and the occasional trip to the doctor to check if all is reasonably OK.

It's also sensible to consider the use of other professional health services, such as physiotherapists and nutritionists to help you with your wellbeing, comfort and physical abilities. They can really help if you engage in a regular programme of care.

In addition, going back to the point above regarding the structure of a working life, there is a lot to be said for maintaining a regular routine in retirement, in whatever form this takes. We've made the point several times so far that an expanse of empty days stretching ahead is not a good way to start retirement, and most people do benefit from some kind of format in their life. Do keep the alarm clock on at a regular time. It can be later, but make sure it gets you up and ready for the day.

And what does your day hold for you? This may be based around exercise, hobbies, academic study, part-time work, volunteering – or a combination of all of these and more. I appreciate that some people like a 'free-form' life, without commitments and with the ability to be entirely spontaneous – however, for most, a modicum of structure at least will be helpful. You don't have to go full control freak, as you may have done at work, and indeed retirement might be a natural point at which you start to learn to let go.

Early death

'The day you draw your pension benefits does not change the day you die'

We've noted this earlier in the book, and perhaps it sounds like a strange statement to make; however, it is undeniably true. You only have a set number of days on this earth. You just don't usually know how long that will be.

For reference, average life expectancy in the UK is dependent on many factors, not least where you live. In a recent measurement period (2018-2020) at the time of writing, average life expectancy at birth in the UK was 79 for males and nearly 83 for females, and at age 65 was 18.5 years for males and 21 years for females (source: Office for National Statistics / ONS). Therefore, you can work out that if you are above average, the likelihood of living to age 85+ is not to be underestimated.

With this in mind, and assuming you're in good health and a non-smoker to start with, you can see that you have a fair probability of reaching a good age and you may well have a couple of decades at least in which to enjoy retirement. This was not always the case, but medical science, diet and a heightened awareness of health issues has helped longevity. However, the figures noted above are only the average, and of course there will be those who pass away earlier or later.

The early death of an individual is hard to deal with, especially if they have just entered retirement. It often seems so unfair that they put all the work in, accumulated enough wealth to enjoy themselves, only to have that chance stolen.

Sometimes one partner is left alone as another dies, leaving all their best laid plans in tatters. Picking up the financial pieces can be cumbersome and time consuming, but it should not be overly difficult, as long as a Will is in place and up to date, and advisors are on hand. However, picking up the emotional pieces can understandably take a lot longer.

The vast majority won't know whether early death is going to strike them or their partner. You can't plan for it in that way – however, you can have your ducks in a row to be as ready as possible if the worst happens. It's the same planning as for a more 'expected' death at an older age – make sure your Will is made and up to date, make sure your family members know where it is, talk with them about what you, and they, might want at the funeral, and what your partner or dependants are most worried about in the event of your death.

It's an awkward subject, and one that has historically been a bit taboo, so sometimes broaching the topic can be tricky. However, it's much better talked about than ignored, as a clear plan and strategy will help those left behind.

Separation and divorce

Working life might have been a blur. Coupled up, a family and pets arrived, homes, career progression made time a sparse commodity, and then the dust began to settle as the offspring went to university, before returning to raid 'the bank of Mum & Dad' to head towards the housing ladder. Not an uncommon pattern for life in the UK. However, separating after all that this part of life had to offer is also not uncommon. Some just feel that they have done enough together and that they would like to start afresh, either alone or with someone new. This applies if you are in a marriage, civil partnership, or any other long-term relationship. You may be aware that the option to apply for a 'no fault' divorce became law in the UK in early April 2022.

For reference, the most recent dataset on divorce from the ONS (ons.gov.uk) notes that there were 103,592 divorces in England and Wales in 2020. Of these divorces, 102,438 were between opposite-sex couples. Overall, this is a decrease of 4.5% compared to 2019. The highest number of opposite-sex divorces recorded was in 2014, when 111,169 divorces were granted in England and Wales. As an additional note, 1,154 divorces between same-sex couples were granted, increasing by 40.4% from 2019. Unreasonable behaviour was the most common reason for divorce across both same-sex and opposite-sex couples in 2020.

To reference the age range focus of this book, which is 50 to 65 years old, according to the ONS the average age for divorce in 2019 was 46.4 for men and 43.9 for women. In line with this, the age group 45 to 49 has the most divorces. However, divorce rates in those aged 60 and over have risen steadily over the years for which data has been collected by the ONS (1950 onwards in this dataset). Taking opposite-sex couples, and using the man's age as an example, in 1950, 627 couples within which the husband was aged 60+ got divorced. In 1970, this was 1,940 couples, in 1990, 5,246 couples and in 2019, 8,322 couples (down from a peak of 9,865 in 2013).

As you start the process of discovering what you might prefer at least the start of retirement to look like, make sure that you share this thought process with your partner. If you don't plan to share the next part of your journey with the person you're with, then now is the time to resolve the outcome amicably. Deferring the issues may only hurt more later.

Individuals considering separation or divorce can look at counselling or mediation, and refer to Keith's book, *Addicted to Wedding Cake*, which is a little dated now, but still clarifies the parameters of what may be involved in the divorce process.

One word: communication

One word will help in this divorce situation: communication. If you want to make your retirement successful, then start communicating. It's vital to manage future expectations, and remember you might have to pay to argue, as I was once told by a legal professional.

If you do start the separation and divorce process, keep it as friendly as you can and get good financial advice on the distribution of assets, particularly if more complex issues such as final salary pensions are involved.

Life's risks

I am not known for being a big risk taker. I have my moments, I can assure you, but if a risk is not well considered and thought through, I am unlikely to be the first in the queue to shout, "Me, me, me!". There are personal risks, and there are business and work risks, and often they intertwine.

You will have faced challenges in your career, and indeed in most aspects of your family and personal life. As a business example, I used to be tested by a senior colleague when they came up with some sales angle to improve profits. If my view was 'no', the project was a goer! Little did I understand at the time that that usually meant that I had to pick up the pieces from their folly, but I soon learned. Indeed, that was the real value I gained: experience and knowledge. Lessons on how not to do something are as valuable as other more positive lessons. I understand that the '40' in the name of the water displacement lubricant WD40 reflects the fact that the fortieth attempt at a formula was successful.

Failing can be a good thing and the process usually stretches the boundaries of understanding and what can personally be achieved. It makes success in whatever measure more satisfying.

Have you considered where you are on the risk scale of life and how this might evolve in retirement? And how will this relate to your planning of your money, health and objectives? Risk is a broad term and will mean different things to different people, as confirmed in my work experiences above. Investment risk with your money is something that can be discussed with a qualified adviser, who will help you to identify your attitude to investment risk and your capacity for loss, in line with your objectives and goals for the future. However, the life risks you take (or avoid) with your health and lifestyle are personal to you – what might be a certain danger to one individual may be a walk in the park to another. Each boundary is a test of your limits.

There's something to be said for applying the investment risk identification process to risks in your personal life. How would you or your family be affected if X happened? If you take up this hobby, what are the worst and best outcomes? How far will your health 'savings' get you or are you running your physical bank account dry already? Will you have enough time?

Be ready to answer these risk questions within yourself, before others do.

Money problems

Having money problems is not an age-related topic and can strike us at any time of our lives. Sticking your head in the sand is often a sure-fire way of exacerbating any financial issue. If you are able, start talking sooner rather than later about money pinch-points. It really is vital not to ignore the situation, especially if you are struggling with debt. There are great organisations, such as Citizens Advice, Step Change and the Debt Advice Foundation, which can help or signpost you to the right place for help. Debt advisers and charities are there to help, not to judge, and they may be able to suggest ways to deal with your money worries that you might not know about.

Talk to your family as well to see if they can help, and if the situation involves a family member rather than yourself, how you can help them? In this latter situation, they may not understand what you have and what you can give, and in the former, honesty and clarity is normally by far the best approach.

Bad habits

You might still hear echoes of your parents chastising you for a bad habit you had picked up as a young child. For me it was biting my nails, which I still do: clearly, I heeded none of their wise words of guidance all those years back.

Now, perhaps the only wisdom you will listen to is your own. The playground of retirement will be new and exciting, but there may be a few bumps on the way. If you spot a new personal bad habit evolving, check you are comfortable with it for your physical and mental wellbeing. You've got this far; you do not want to find that you go off the rails at this enjoyable part of your life.

There are of course good habits, such as stretching the mind on daily basis. Some swear by completing the daily Sudoku game, crossword, or now perhaps Wordle, to keep the mind agile: all good disciplines within retirement routines to keep the brain active and supple.

Positive outcomes ahead

Fairly, it might be suggested that this is not the most positive of chapters within this book. Life throws up challenges both large and small. Many can be brushed away with ease. Others, as we have seen, can cause greater concerns. We hope that we have caged these potential troubles within one chapter, but not caged your enthusiasm to solve any problems that arise and to move forward in your retirement.

Your nudge notes:

Coming in to Land — Runway to Retirement
Chapter 9: What's going to stop you?

<u>Your thoughts and views</u>

• You've made it to the arrivals carousel of retirement? What is going to stop you having the time of your life?

• Are there others who may alter your progress to the retirement you want? Can you quantify this (e.g. dependants needing money)?

• What have you taken from this chapter to suggest that you might have to make changes?

- Have you talked to your family about death and the plans you have put in place if all goes wrong and where everything is stored? If not, get talking soon to ensure a failsafe is ready.

- Are there any quick wins or adjustments available to you to achieve more for your retirement now?

- Have you booked that medical? Do it now!

- Write one action that you will now implement.

10. And relax...if you can afford to

Hopefully, you've now got a plan, it's agreed between you and your loved ones, and now you have to implement it.

Often, and certainly when it comes to retirement planning, actions can speak louder than words. Returning to the often-asked question, 'Am I going to be OK?', with a prepared mind and attitude, and some good money planning, the answer is likely to be affirmative, although managing expectations is important. Maslow's hierarchy of needs springs to mind, with the preferred aim of being close to, or at the top of the triangle of human needs. You might have worn out the life wallpaper that you used as the canvas for your plans and have now rolled this up to enjoy the year ahead before reviewing again.

Staying sharp, wherever you live

And is there now a standard age to retire? In the UK, 65 seemed to be the age that most would hang up their occupational attire and stop work. I thought I would look at other countries to see if there was a significant difference elsewhere. A survey by Schroders in 2017 suggests that somewhere around age 65-68 seems to be about standard now irrespective of where you live in the world. But will you stay as sharp as you once were?

As you get older, you may become more cautious in your outlook, but not less sharp according to a recent study from Heidelberg University in Germany. Indeed, and to some extent reassuringly, the study published in February 2022 indicates that the brain between the ages of 30 and 60 remains sharp. The large-scale sample of 1.2 million people, aged 10 to 80, found mental speed remained relatively stable between 30 and 60, noting that caution tended to increase with age from 18 to 65.

The researchers undertook a survey that showed participants a series of online images and asked them to place them in two categories - good and bad – through the press of a button. Mathematical models were then used to estimate the speed at which participants completed their tasks. They confirmed their findings in the publication *Nature Human Behaviour*.

It is reassuring that the scientists note that although the average time to complete the overall task slowed after the age of 20, the mental speed of processing information did not start to slow until 60. Plenty of time then to get your head around your retirement plans as you make your approach to the release from work.

This is likely to be quite a journey. It's your life, but are you ready?

Only 1 in 5 took professional advice. That's appalling!

The objective of this book is to make a positive difference to readers' retirement outcomes, even if that is to consider the positives and negatives of the actions that can be taken and to dismiss some of them. Many individuals take no professional advice or guidance and make uninformed choices from the perhaps limited options put before them. Survey results in February 2022 by abrdn showed that only 22% of UK savers took advice on their retirement planning, whilst ironically 48% were worried about running out of money in retirement. Just over 1 in 5 took professional advice. That's appalling!

A reflection on our profession in part for sure, but also a reflection perhaps on individuals' own understanding that there is choice, and lots of it. You can normally make a positive impact on your plans and the benefits you receive if you take a look.

However you seek to gain some guidance or advice, don't be shy. It doesn't matter if you have piles of cash, or a small pot. Positive differences can normally be made. I hope that this book will inspire you to take action.

If you have the choice of timing: sunshine

Some folk plan ahead. Tell me something you did not know. But my question to you is how far in advance do you plan? Hopefully a good few years.

In this paragraph, I am not referring to at what age, or the age range within which you plan to retire. I am referring to the month you retire, if you have the choice. We have noted this in chapter 9, but I think it's worth reiterating. Many people can time when they resign or retire, and I think there is nothing worse than retiring in the late autumn, when the nights start to get dark and cold. You can certainly book a holiday or two, but you will likely return to the cold and damp of the UK. Seasonal affective disorder, or SAD, can be quite serious for some.

The end of the tax year is 05 April each year and it can be good to think about ending work around that point. The weather is getting warmer, and you can cap out your earnings in one tax year and start your retirement income in the next. Almost a line in the sand from a tax perspective for the transition from work to retirement.

If you struggle to settle into retirement, at least you can sit in the garden or park in the warmth of the summer sunshine ahead and think further about what retirement and the opportunity it offers means to you. Many have enjoyed this timing option and I think it is a really good springboard into the start of your new life.

Say no to a paint brush in the first six months

Many look at 'futureproofing' their home to be ready for retirement so that you don't have to spend the first six months of the release from the shackles of work decorating or fixing things at your home. These issues should usually have been corrected years ago, but you never really had time to get round to it. Work and life just happened, and you know 'this or that' needed doing, it's just probably got a lot worse through benign neglect. And we all know how difficult it is to get a good, reasonably priced handyman to actually turn up these days. Not their fault, just a shortage of skills in the UK, and that's a whole different conversation.

I am not referring here to making changes to aid mobility and access as examples, although vital if needed. From the feedback from some people, they are more often referring to a new bathroom and kitchen, a small extension, or a full redecoration to welcome in a new start not only for them, but also for the environment that they live in. I was once asked if my house was my 'forever home'. I don't believe that one exists for me, but I think I am the exception rather than the rule. And if you are in your mid 70's as an example, and you are contemplating a move, is the property you are considering what you've always wanted for your retirement? If you aren't planning a move, are you definitely in your 'forever home'? If not, now is the time to make it happen, before it gets too difficult from a health or fitness point of view.

If you have used the timing to retire into the summer, you will be outdoors anyway, filling your time with all things sunny, which you could never do when you were working. That well-earned two-day weekend stint grabbing a tan in the garden or park has changed. Guess what? You can now go every day of the week if you like!

Bank of Mum & Dad

Our financial comments and life-learnings are nearly at an end. Some might sigh in relief. One of the unknowns financially is how and when you might be called on to support the family with money and lump sums, if at all. It is a conundrum in itself as, we admit, was where to fit this topic into the book, noting the connection to retirement funds.

Retirement is a life junction both for you as an individual, but also as a couple if you are in a relationship, and as a family if you have dependants. We regularly hear from clients and other contacts that even when a child has left home, this does not mean that they are no longer dependent. 'As financially independent as they are ever going to become' has been used to describe the situation, and we often find that parents are keen to help their adult children on to the property ladder, or supplement their income, or pay for school fees for grandchildren, as examples. You may not know that even grandchildren can now start pension savings from their infancy, usually funded by parents or grandparents, although you may not be around for them to say thanks!

Higher final earnings or the release of pension tax-free cash, with your own debts repaid and suitable assets available elsewhere, might be a good source of help for dependants. If tax free cash becomes available from pension arrangements, and is not needed to maintain your own lifestyle, this may be an opportunity to distribute funds to younger generations. The cascading of wealth is not uncommon, but care is needed as to how it is achieved, and it is recommended that any gifting is documented and that gift allowances for inheritance tax purposes are used where available. One point of note is that there should be no pressure to gift funds away through any kind of wealth transfer to younger generations.

One of the biggest lenders in the UK over recent years has been from family help, affectionately known by many as 'The Bank of Mum & Dad' (or BOMAD for short, which is not very affectionate). To put this into context the property group Savills noted at the end of 2021 that parents supported 49% of first-time buyer purchases in that year. Total contributions from parents helping younger generations to buy a house were expected to reach around £9.8 billion in 2021. Just when you have a bit of cash, the kids want to get it from you!

We have seen some use of emotional pressure to obtain funds from parents and grandparents which is not pleasant to witness. Take individual advice, but if it doesn't feel right, don't do it.

I really wanted to know them

We have spoken to many children who are saddened that they did not know more about their parents' real life before they passed away or, to some extent even worse, they lost capacity through the horrors of dementia or other cognitive declines. They really wish that they had asked them to lay out a few pages of their life to give more of a picture of what their life was really like. Simply, to know them better. Sure, there are records of births, death, marriages, and children, along with trades or professions, perhaps with the odd location thrown in, but do these really tell you anything more? If you are able, write out a resumé of your life story and give it to a child or relative. It may reveal more to them than was ever obvious or was perhaps just covered by the sands of time. If it's not for your children, do it for the next generation. Someone in your family will want to know more.

Just another retirement book?

There was, and is, the risk that this is 'just another retirement book'. We feel that having focused on pre-retirement, from the age of 50 to 60, and then the initial phase of retirement. With the age range of 60 to around 65/70 years old, this book provides real insight into what needs to be considered on the often-emotional journey to finally stopping work, or at least reducing your workload and the associated responsibility.

The nuggets of information and financial thoughts throughout the pages we hope will add depth to the often asked and very natural question, 'Will I be OK?'. Don't feel alone: many others are going through the same thought processes as you at any time. The numbers are massive, and you might have guessed we like a stat or two, as you will see.

One website, Statista.com, in its report on the population of England in 2020, by age group, suggests that just over 10.8 million people fell into the age range category (50-64) in 2020, and 13.6 million people in total if you extend the range to age 69. Interestingly, the age range of 50-54 is the most of any age group, with 3.875 million people in the group, and certainly a focus group for this text.

Setting the title of the book as Coming in to Land seems ever more appropriate when looking at this data and the target groups for the text. It's clear that there are many millions who will be approaching their individual runway to retirement.

We also thought that this book would stand the test of time over the next decade as these age groups move forward and begin to enjoy their newly found freedom. There is clearly much work to do for the significant numbers that will retire over the years immediately ahead. Legislation might also interfere with retirement plans as the minimum age for drawing pension benefits increases.

What really counts?

Take time and speak with friends and colleagues to get their view on the prospects ahead and the way they plan to accomplish their retirement aspirations. If they have none, perhaps you can share a few of yours as inspiration to others. Also, take advice from professionals where needed. Some people are very well versed on their planning and financial situation, and that's great. Getting a second opinion, even if it confirms what you already know, may not take long and will as a minimum add more confidence to the opportunities at hand.

Most of all, enjoy the journey from start to finish. You may well never make this journey again and you are old enough and wise enough to know what ticks your boxes.

It is an honour for us to help people retire, and an honour to share their journeys. We hope that the pages of this book will give you focus and conviction to get the most out of the fulfilling years ahead.

Conclusion

Retirement is a life junction
Promise yourself you will make it happen

Achieving stuff in your life is important. You might have thought that you stopped achieving a long time ago, but you haven't. It just feels a bit like crawling through treacle sometimes to reach the next goal. As suggested in the introduction, well done for getting this far!

We also know that pensions are a particularly dry topic, and it can be difficult for many to get animated about getting the best from your accumulated wealth. It's really important, so persevere please.

Retirement is a scary word for many – for most it means to withdraw from work. Somehow, it can also imply that you are withdrawing from more things than work, indeed from many aspects of life. That's simply not true. It is actually a new beginning, and time for you to enjoy everything you have worked so hard for.

Let's take a step back to look forward:

- Do you remember applying for your first job? How you tidied yourself up to sit in front of your soon-to-be boss to impress them?
- Do you remember blowing your first pay on something you always wanted, that seemed so important at the time, but now just elicits a chuckle?

- Do you remember scrimping and saving to claw together every penny you could to buy your first property?
- Do you remember getting married and feeling that you were about to own the world ahead?
- Do you remember the birth of your first child and promising them everything?
- Perhaps, do you remember getting divorced and promising yourself that you would recover and make life better?
- Perhaps you may remember receiving an inheritance and, with a reflective tear in your eye, realising that this is a life changing amount?

Each was a life junction personal to you, and your retirement is no different. It is another of your life junctions.

You had to strive to achieve the events listed above and planning to retire is no different. You have to promise yourself you will do your best, and that starts with planning.

Please don't do it for someone else: do it for you. Twenty or thirty years of retirement is a long time to contemplate why you messed up at the final hurdle. Conversely, it's also a long time to really, really enjoy yourself.

Pick your life junction direction and run with it. You owe this one to yourself.

Make it happen!

Your nudge notes:

Coming in to Land — Runway to Retirement
Chapter 10: And relax...if you can afford to

Your thoughts and views

• You're at your retirement party. Are you where you wanted and expected to be?

• What would you tell your twenty years younger self to do differently if you had the chance?

• Who can you speak with to share your retirement plans and swap notes on what they plan?

- What's the first thing on your retirement list that you are going to enjoy? And why?

- How will you review your plans in retirement as they evolve, and what time period will you set?

- Write one action that you will now implement.

Epilogue

Thank you for reading our experiences of what points and issues have counted to individuals as they have retired over the decades. We have been honoured to share their journeys.

Keith:

Writing for me is a very cathartic process. It allows me to place into text what runs through my mind as an individual, as a business owner, a husband, and a financial planner. I was inspired by the topic for this book and was able to create the core of the text within about three weeks, during the cold dark nights of the month of January. My first book took six months, and I was just as inspired at the time a decade plus ago. The difference now is the wisdom and methodology that has been developed over the years of writing.

Vicky:

I very much enjoy writing; in fact, it's one of my favourite aspects of our work. Being involved in a book that pulls together what we do every day for clients who are coming up to or entering retirement has been a fascinating exercise. It has highlighted how complex pension planning can be, and how important it is to get it right at the outset.

Both:

We hope that the inspiration we both felt whilst writing this book is reflected in the ideas, situations and experiences that we have woven into the chapters to help others think about what might be on the horizon. Hopefully you have seen that there is much to embrace in the next few years as you come into land on the runway of your retirement. Perhaps not straight away, but on the horizon for sure. We hope it's not too bumpy or turbulent a ride and landing, and that your luggage appears on the correct carousel. You might have to 'buckle up' for the financial and emotional ride, and we are advocates of starting your personal journey early.

Although important, it's not all about the money. It's about the experiences, people, events and places that you want to base yourself around as you start the approach to retirement, and the first retirement phase of your time away from work. The 'active years' should be fun! Are you excited by the prospect? You should be, although we appreciate it might be a bit daunting at the outset.

We also know that planning the money you will need for retirement is not the most exciting of topics, but it is fundamentally necessary. You might think of it as tedious, boring, or technical, but planning the cash for what you are going to do, and with whom, is inspiring as you enter perhaps the most important phase of an individual's life. You might just book a month of sleep to catch up, as soon as work stops, but don't worry, the plans of what to do with your now vast free time will come thick and fast. If the middle money sections of this book give you a heads-up to what could be achieved, or if there is not enough cash to go round, then the bite-size chunks of money information should be slightly more palatable now when you look at your own position. They should help with the question, 'Am I going to be OK?'.

With childhood, initial education and a working life having been achieved, and hopefully ill-health and death a good two decades away, if not more, this next fifteen, twenty, thirty years ahead should be epic, if you want them to be. It's great to know that the choice of what you do is in your gift.

Our goal was to get your brain ticking as to what needs to be achieved and to help manage expectations as to what can actually be done. Like life, retirement is an evolution, therefore any plans you make will need to be regularly reviewed, and of course on many occasions life has a habit of going off course. It would be naïve to think that the path through your retirement will be without its issues. Life, health, wellbeing and family might get in the way to cause trouble, perhaps when you least need it. Just when you think it's looking great, something might just crop up. It's all part of life's rich and diverse tapestry.

If you are one of those who plans to work through your retirement, then enjoy your time. I may well join you in the ranks and I look forward to it. I enjoy what I do, and if you share that continued passion for your work, I salute you. However, I don't think that I could have written this book until I had reached an age when the topic became far more relevant to my life phase than before. Having reached the age of 55 by the time this book was published, the whole process has become far more real and tangible than it was in the past.

Talking and advising on the topic is one thing. Being of an age to be able to implement changes if I wanted to is an entirely different position. I personally will not be pressing any retirement buttons anytime soon; I enjoy helping others reach their retirement goals and aspirations. It is somehow enlightening to know however that the window is now open. A personal milestone? Perhaps not, but definitely a life junction, should one care to take it.

As a financial planner, it is noteworthy to observe the statistics of the wave of people who will plan to retire in the next decade is significant. It reminds me of the 'bulge years' in school classroom sizes way back when. A busy decade ahead beckons, and I look forward to the challenges this presents.

And for you, in retirement, what are you going to do with the most valuable commodity known to humankind, namely time? I hope you will have aspirations to pursue your favoured pastime or hobby, whatever it may be, when you reach the status of retiree. And if you have not got a particular passion or interest, now is the time to go and discover it. Get yourself some likes, loves and dislikes before retirement is on your doorstep.

We have also looked with anticipation at the good bits, and as a balance, touched on the realities of entering retirement. We have spoken to many who have retired who say that they don't know how they managed to fit work into their lives, they are so busy, and, importantly, fulfilled. It fills us with pride that perhaps, in a small way, we have allowed them to be so happy. Please don't be shy of your plans and make this next phase of your life the best so far.

Whatever you do, the important stuff in your life, your family, friends, passions will not change irrespective of whether you work, or retire, or achieve a mixture of the two. Hold close what you value, and don't let the noise of life distract you from what is important to you.

Work hard to get the cornerstones of your retirement dream in place promptly, whilst you are coming into land on your retirement runway. When you have done that, make sure you enjoy yourself as often as you can. The shackles of work are gone, along with the structure work provided, and this new time is not going to repeat itself. We've mentioned bad habits, and you will know what they are for you. Keep them under control where you can to get the most out of what you do each day when work becomes a distant memory.

We wish you a long, happy, and healthy retirement, with enough money to make it happen. You worked so hard to get here, burning the midnight oil on many occasions. We hope that you do the same again now, but this time having huge fun and adventure throughout your days, and long into the night.

Remember, you don't have to get up in the morning. Enjoy!

No financial advice of any description is offered or deemed to have been provided within the text of this book. Seek financial advice from a qualified adviser for your own individual needs.

No legal advice is given or provided within this text and you should refer to your legal adviser for specific information about your needs and requirements.

Some detail in the text of this book is based on the tax regime applicable to the UK in the tax year 2022/2023. Legislation for tax and allowances can and does change over time.

Economic factors vary constantly. These can include returns, inflation, exchange rates, commodity values, legislation and tax to name only a few. Any indicated returns in the pages of this book are examples only and they will vary over time.

Seek individual guidance, advice and updates for your own circumstances and arrangements.

Reference pages

Introduction

- National population projections, Office for National Statistics, published January 2022:
  https://www.ons.gov.uk/
  peoplepopulationandcommunity/
  populationandmigration/populationprojections/bulletins/
  nationalpopulationprojections/2020basedinterim

- Retirement Living Standards report, Pensions and Lifetime Savings Association and Loughborough University, published October 2021:
  https://www.retirementlivingstandards.org.uk/

Chapter 1

- Population of England in 2020, by age group, Statista:
  https://www.statista.com/statistics/281208/population-of-the-england-by-age-group/

- Movements out of work for those aged over 50 years since the start of the coronavirus pandemic, Office for National Statistics, published March 2022:
  https://www.ons.gov.uk/employmentandlabourmarket/
  peopleinwork/employmentandemployeetypes/articles/
  movementsoutofworkforthoseagedover50yearssincethest
  artofthecoronaviruspandemic/2022-03-14

Chapter 3

- Sixty the most popular age to retire early, Aviva, published December 2021:
  https://www.aviva.com/newsroom/news-releases/
  2021/12/sixty-the-most-popular-age-to-retire-early/

Chapter 5

- Protecting pension savers - Five years on from the Pension Freedoms: Accessing pension savings, Work & Pensions Committee, published January 2022:
  https://publications.parliament.uk/pa/cm5802/cmselect/
  cmworpen/237/report.html

Chapter 7

- Population estimates for the UK, England and Wales, Scotland and Northern Ireland: mid-2020, Office for National Statistics, published June 2021:
  https://www.ons.gov.uk/
  peoplepopulationandcommunity/
  populationandmigration/populationestimates/bulletins/
  annualmidyearpopulationestimates/mid2020

- National Pension Tracing Day:
  https://nationalpensiontracingday.co.uk/

Chapter 9

- Covid early retirees top 3 million in US, Bloomberg, October 2021:
  https://www.bloomberg.com/news/articles/2021-10-22/
  covid-early-retirees-top-3-million-in-u-s-fed-research-
  show

- Pandemic polarises retirement gap for over 50s, Legal & General, March 2021: https://group.legalandgeneral.com/en/newsroom/press-releases/pandemic-polarises-retirement-opportunity-gap-for-over-50s

- National life tables, Office for National Statistics, published September 2021: https://www.ons.gov.uk/peoplepopulationandcommunity/birthsdeathsandmarriages/lifeexpectancies/bulletins/nationallifetablesunitedkingdom/2018to2020
- Divorces in England and Wales: 2020, Office for National Statistics, published February 2022: https://www.ons.gov.uk/peoplepopulationandcommunity/birthsdeathsandmarriages/divorce/bulletins/divorcesinenglandandwales/2020

Chapter 10

- World pension ages on the rise: when will you retire, Schroders, published November 2017: https://www.schroders.com/en/uk/adviser/insights/retirement/world-pension-ages-on-the-rise-when-will-you-retire/

- Mental speed is high until age 60 as revealed by analysis of over a million participants, published in the journal *Nature Human Behaviour*, in February 2022, and referenced in a BBC article in February 2022: https://www.nature.com/articles/s41562-021-01282-7 https://www.bbc.co.uk/news/health-60431986

- Retirees urged to consider advice as new research highlights stark advice gap, abrdn, published February 2022: https://www.abrdn.com/corporate/media-centre/media-centre-news-article/retirees-urged-to-consider-advice-as-new-research-highlights-stark-advice-gap

- Bank of Mum & Dad to hit record high in 2021 with a £10 billion handout, Savills, published October 2021: https://www.savills.com/insight-and-opinion/savills-news/320635/bank-of-mum-and-dad-to-hit-record-high-in-2021-with-a-%C2%A310-billion-handout

- Population of England in 2020, by age group, Statista: https://www.statista.com/statistics/281208/population-of-the-england-by-age-group/

About the authors

About Keith Churchouse

Keith was rather born into financial services, with his father Roger being a bank manager for many years. With over 36 years of experience within financial services in various guises, Keith started his own business in Guildford, Surrey in 2004.

As a Chartered Financial Planner, Keith holds a degree in financial services and his dulcet tones have been heard on BBC local radio for over 17 years providing financial thoughts, ideas and opinion to listeners. Great fun to do!

In his spare time, where he can, he renovates old cars, usually early 1970s models, reflecting the first time he fell in love with all things four wheeled, and then subsequently two wheeled. In fact, anything capable of being motorised. The main attraction now is the tangibility of being able to build something that can be seen, felt and experienced when complete.

Dealing with facts and figures in the day job is very enjoyable but making a real gain on a spreadsheet or fund choice is not usually tangible. This creativity works in both areas, but one can be parked on a drive, and one on a pension summary table.

About Vicky Fulcher

Following a career in environmental technology, Vicky switched into the financial services industry in early 2014, joining the team at Chapters Financial in Guildford as a Trainee Financial Planner. Vicky chose to study some of the financial planning profession's exams prior to joining to ensure that she had the aptitude for and interest in what can be a complicated subject.

Her successful career within the team has seen Vicky promoted to director level over the last few years, having completed further exams in the process. Many will know that studying whilst working at the same time can be a significant burden to carry. Her experience of retirement planning over the years has grown, and she enjoys working with Keith to provide advice in this topical and ever-growing area.

Outside work, family life is hectic and rewarding.

Working together

Keith and Vicky have worked together for eight years at their Chartered Financial Planning business in Guildford, Surrey. Considering views, opinions and experiences on client case work over the many years of business, it is good to share some of this collective wisdom within the pages of this book.

Milton Keynes UK
Ingram Content Group UK Ltd.
UKHW020026160823
426897UK00013B/186